THE CONSCIOUS LUCK WORKBOOK

THE CONSCIOUS LUCK WORKBOOK

APPLYING THE EIGHT SECRETS TO INTENTIONALLY CHANGE YOUR FORTUNE

GAY HENDRICKS,
CAROL KLINE,
and KAMIN SAMUEL

Waterside Productions

Copyright © 2020 Gay Hendricks, Carol Kline, and Kamin Samuel.

All rights reserved. This book or any portion thereof may not be reproduced or used in any manner whatsoever without the express written permission of the publisher except for the use of brief quotations in a book review.

ISBN-13: 978-1-951805-33-3 print edition
ISBN-13: 978-1-951805-34-0 EBOOK EDITION

Waterside Press
2055 Oxford Ave.
Cardiff, CA 92007
www.waterside.com

CONTENTS

Preface

Part One

Getting Started

Part Two

Deepening Your Experience of the Eight Secrets

Part Three

Incorporating Luck into Your Daily Life

Conscious Luck Resources

Preface

A Message from Gay Hendricks

I'm happy and grateful to present to you a genuine labor of love, the new *Conscious Luck Workbook*!

When *Conscious Luck* was published and given a warm reception by our readers, Carol and I created the Conscious Luck Global Community on Facebook, a gathering place for luck enthusiasts to connect and discuss this empowering new perspective on intentionally creating good fortune. The Community is growing by the day, its popularity fueled mainly by the stories people share of how their luck is increasing.

The Community has also yielded another treasure: the deep insights and questions raised by its members. As we responded to the questions, we began to think of new activities and processes that would be useful. The glimmer of an idea to create a workbook began to form in our minds.

Then, a genuine example of Conscious Luck came along: enter the third member of our team, a consultant and coach I'd known and admired for many years, Kamin Samuel. What I didn't know was that in her work with executives and organizations, Kamin had a great deal of experience in creating workbooks! Kamin and Carol went into high gear and now you're holding the result, something I believe you'll find most useful.

In the following pages, you'll discover one activity after another that will free up your mind, light up your heart, and give you a boost on your journey to being the luckiest person on earth. These ingeniously simple processes are designed to make it even easier to implement the concepts in *Conscious Luck*.

Remember, though, the processes only work if you do them. I urge you to sit down in a quiet place and complete every single exercise in the Workbook, giving each one your full attention and responding from a deeply honest place inside you.

The quality of your life—and mine—is determined by our openness to learning. Open your mind and plunge into these life-changing practices. Claim all the luck that's yours, then pass it on to the people around you.

I want to live in a world where each one of us feels like the luckiest person on earth. If that's the kind of world you want to live in too, jump right in and start getting luckier right now.

Gay Hendricks
September 2020

PART ONE

Getting Started

Launching Your Luck

Welcome to the *Conscious Luck Workbook*! We're thrilled that you're taking this next, oh-so-important step on your Conscious Luck journey!

This workbook is a companion to the original *Conscious Luck* book and will help you own and apply the principles of Conscious Luck more fully. Since it builds on the original book, we recommend you use this workbook *after* reading *Conscious Luck* or, if you'd like, *while* you read it.

The *Conscious Luck Workbook* is also meant to be *your* companion—a friend who links arms with you to guide, encourage, and support you on your path. Think of it this way: using the workbook is like working with us—Gay, Carol, and Kamin—as your coaches, to make Conscious Luck a living, breathing reality in your life.

We were inspired to create the workbook after many *Conscious Luck* readers told us that they

- were writing notes in the margins of the book and needed more space to process their reflections and insights,
- wanted to deepen the release of their personal barriers to luck, and
- were eager to learn how to make the eight Secrets come alive in their day-to-day experiences.

This workbook will help you do all three!

Before you dive into the workbook, you'll want to complete the Conscious Luck Self-Assessment Tool and Focus Guide, if you haven't already done that. You can find it at https://www.consciousluck.com/conscious-luck-self-assessment-tool-and-focus-guide. This tool will tell you how much Conscious Luck you're currently creating for yourself, and help you decide which Conscious Luck Secret(s) you'll want to focus on most.

Off the Page and into Your Life

Self-help books work. But only if you do.
— Matt Sandrini, business and entrepreneurship coach

We've all experienced it: You read a personal development book that's brilliant, compelling, inspiring, and yet your life doesn't really change. That's because it's one thing to read something—even have an *a-ha* moment—and quite another to apply what you've learned to your unique personality, conditioning, and life experience, and then take action.

This workbook will help you dive more deeply into the ideas and practices you learned in *Conscious Luck*. Using the exercises and journaling, you'll gain insights into how your specific patterns of thinking and behaving influence your ability to use each Secret. Then, based on what you discover, you'll find ways to boost that Secret's power in your life.

And because changing old habits can be challenging—it's called a *comfort* zone for a reason—we've included accountability and tracking tools that will make new, more luck-creating attitudes and behaviors feel like second nature to you.

Practicing the Conscious Luck Secrets—not occasionally, but consistently over time—will develop the neural pathways for new, lucky habits that lead to a life of abundance, love, and success.

A final note about how you can get the most benefit from this workbook: It's not enough to think about change or even intend to change. True and lasting transformation requires action. There's a great story that illustrates this point.

Picture the scene: There are five birds sitting on a telephone wire. Three of them decide to fly south. How many are left? If you said two, guess again. The correct answer is five.

Deciding to fly south is not the same thing as actually *doing* it. To accomplish anything, you've got to connect your intention to action. So go ahead, *decide* to complete this workbook—and then *do* it! We'll be cheering you on.

The first step is refreshing your memory about exactly what we mean by "luck."

Defining Luck: Getting on the Same Page

In *Conscious Luck*, we offer a totally new way to look at luck—one that turns the conventional understandings of the term on their head. Let's take a minute to examine those understandings.

The most popular definition of any word is usually found in the dictionary. Here's the *Cambridge Dictionary* definition of luck: "the force that causes things, especially good things, to happen to you by chance and not as a result of your own efforts or abilities."

If you ask people what luck is, most connect it to gambling: slot machines, poker, horse races, or playing the lottery. For many people, luck is associated with superstition and magical thinking (in the unhealthy sense)—for example, carrying lucky charms and finding four-leaf clovers. Others understand luck as serendipity or random chance. Still others, with a more scientific outlook, think that events simply happen based on cause and effect, and that luck is just a subjective label people use to make sense of those events.

In the world of religion, luck has both negative and positive associations. Some religious people don't believe in luck at all—whatever happens is God's will, and any other explanation is considered "the devil's work." For others, luck is one of God's blessings, experienced as feeling favored or receiving grace or divine providence.

The common thread in all of these is that luck is an external force that's random and beyond our control. And it's this interpretation that's shaped—and limited—our experience of luck for centuries.

What Does Luck Mean to *You*?

Here's where your personal participation starts! Actively applying all that you learned in *Conscious Luck* begins with the following exercise and journaling. Please don't skip them. If you haven't got a pen or pencil handy, please take a moment now to find one. Then, after taking some time to ask yourself the questions in the exercise and explore your own mind and heart, write out your answers. For the fastest progress, give these exercises—and all the ones that follow—your best shot.

Exercise: Your Definition of Luck

Most of us have a general notion of what luck is, but we might never have really asked ourselves what we mean *specifically* when we use that term. It's time to remedy that.

Ask yourself: *What does "luck" mean to me?* Can you remember what luck meant to you before reading *Conscious Luck*? Do you remember your initial reaction to the title? Write your answers in the space below:

____

____

____

____

____

____

____

Take a Moment to Reflect: Where does your definition of luck come from? Whose voice is that? What were you taught about luck—if anything—growing up? In the space below, write down any answers that come up for you:

____

____

____

____

Now that we've explored what the dictionary, most people, and you in particular have to say about luck, let's do a short review of the key principles you learned in *Conscious Luck*.

Our Definition of Luck

In *Conscious Luck*, we define luck as an ever-present force that you can harness consciously to flourish on all levels of life—mentally, emotionally, physically, and financially.

Although there will always be an element of chance to luck—both good and bad—research in the field of Positive Psychology and the experiences of consistently lucky people show that a great deal of your luck can be changed, and quickly, with some conscious attention on your part.

Just as there are rules for improving your health—get enough sleep, eat a balanced, fresh diet, stay hydrated, exercise regularly—there are specific guidelines for improving your luck.

We love the analogy Stanford University professor, Dr. Tina Seelig, uses to explain this: "Luck is rarely a lightning strike—isolated and dramatic—but a wind that blows constantly . . . You need to build a sail—made up of certain tiny behaviors—to catch the winds of luck."

The eight Conscious Luck Secrets provide the step-by-step instructions for building that sail and harnessing the winds of luck.

Reading *Conscious Luck* started your journey to intentional good fortune and using the tools in the following pages will accelerate that process. When you fully integrate the eight Secrets into your daily life, you can't help but be luckier.

Take a Moment to Reflect: Thinking about our definition of luck, what comes up for you? Do you feel any resistance, or doubt? Do you feel hopeful? Are you excited about having more luck in your life?

10 Defining Luck

How to Use the Conscious Luck Workbook

The workbook is divided into three parts and a Resources section:

Part 1: Getting Started

So far in Part 1, we've shared the purpose of this workbook and asked you to clarify your definition of luck. Next, you'll find out how to get the most from the exercises, journaling, tracking, and resources that follow.

Part 2: Deepening Your Experience of the Eight Secrets

In Part 2, you'll explore each of the eight Conscious Luck Secrets from many different angles, "trying on" the Secret to see how it "fits" and more importantly, where it needs tailoring to address your specific situation and needs.

Each chapter in Part 2 includes exercises designed to focus your attention on the most significant aspects of the Secret being explored. Some of the exercises are written, others are eyes-closed processes, and there are a couple that have a whole-body element to them. In addition, there are journaling sections where you'll be asked to reflect on your experiences during the exercises, or on questions we pose, and then write down whatever thoughts, insights, and feelings come up for you.

Please keep in mind that there are no right or wrong answers, and no need to try to be perfect. Simply give yourself the freedom to be open and authentic—*whatever* that looks like—in service to living a luckier life.

Throughout Part 2, you'll be instructed to take long, slow, deep breaths we call *belly-breaths* to bring your attention to your belly as you breathe. Often, when people are told to take a deep breath, they raise their shoulders and upper chest as they inhale to make room for the larger amount of air they're taking in. But lifting the shoulders on a deep breath doesn't have the same calming, centering effect that breathing into the belly does, so it's important to be conscious of what's happening in your body as you breathe.

If you're not familiar with belly-breathing, it's easy to learn. Whenever you see the instruction to take deep belly-breaths, do the following:

1. As you start inhaling (through your nose), make a conscious effort to pull the air all the way down to the bottom of your lungs—as if you're breathing into your belly area. If you're doing it correctly, you'll feel your belly expand outward, away from the spine. (While you're learning, feel free to rest your hand on your belly as you breathe in. You should feel the belly pushing your hand forward, away from the spine.)
2. As you continue the inhale, let the in-breath expand your rib-cage area and finally your chest. Imagine you're pouring water into a pitcher, filling the pitcher from the bottom to the top. When you correctly take a belly-breath inhale, your shoulders don't lift at all.
3. As you exhale (through your nose), immediately start squeezing the breath out from the very bottom part of your lungs, firmly pulling the belly inward toward the spine. If you're resting your hand on your belly, you should feel the belly pulling in beneath your hand, moving toward the spine.
4. As you continue the exhale, contract your rib-cage area and then your chest, pressing the air upward and out through your nose. Imagine you're squeezing a tube of toothpaste, applying pressure, starting at the bottom and continuing in a smooth movement toward the top.
5. When you finish exhaling, rest quietly for a second or two before beginning the next inhale. With belly-breaths, you always start the breaths, both in and out, by moving the belly. On an inhale, the belly bulges out, and on an exhale, the belly pulls in.
6. One complete breath—an inhale and exhale—should take <u>at least</u> 6–8 seconds: 3–4 seconds to breathe in completely and 3–4 seconds to breathe out. Everyone is different, so experiment until you find the count that's comfortable and relaxing for you.

Some people find it easier to learn to belly-breathe while lying on their back. If you'd like, feel free to go through the steps above lying down.

For more in-depth instructions, go to the Resources section, where you'll find a link to a video of Gay demonstrating how to belly-breathe.

Part 3: Incorporating Luck into Your Daily Life

In Part 3, you'll find two tracking tools to help you schedule and record your daily Conscious Luck activities. Studies have shown that whatever you focus on expands, so focusing on luck each day will increase your luck significantly.

The first tracking tool is the 21-Day Luck Activation Journal, to use as you work your way through Part 2 of this workbook. Scientists believe it takes 21 days to form a new habit, which is why we've created a 21-day journal. Make a commitment to use the journal every day and very soon those lucky behaviors will become part of your routine.

The 21-Day Luck Activation Journal has one page for each day that includes the Morning and Evening Luck Activation Meditations, spaces to write out your Conscious Luck commitments and any lucky events from the day, and a section to capture what you're grateful for. ***Please start using the 21-Day Luck Activation Journal as soon as you begin Part 2.***

The second tracking tool is the 30-Day Lucky Life Tracker, which you'll use *after* you've completed Part 2. It's designed to anchor your new habits of consciously creating and living a luckier life every day.

The 30-Day Tracker has two pages for each day: one to be filled out in the morning, and one in the evening. It includes the same Morning and Evening Luck Activation Meditations and the daily rewriting of your Conscious Luck commitment and luck inventory that are in the 21-Day Journal. There are also additional luck-boosting practices—related to the Secrets—to track. ***As soon as you complete Part 2, please begin using the 30-Day Tracker.***

More information, as well as detailed instructions for using both tracking tools, can be found in Part 3.

Conscious Luck Resources

In this section, you'll find additional materials to support you on your Conscious Luck journey, including links to the resources on the Conscious Luck Workbook web page, which contains all the meditation audio recordings, downloadable tracker and journal pages, additional information and videos on essence pace and belly-breathing, and links to connect with the Global Conscious Luck Community.

The Resources section also has a blank page where you can write out all of the eight Secrets yourself, as recommended at the end of *Conscious Luck*, or if you prefer, you can color in a preprinted Eight Secrets page (think adult coloring book!) that's provided here in the workbook. Or you can download the preprinted Eight Secrets poster as a PDF through a link on the website.

At the very end of the workbook, there's a NOTES section with blank pages for you to write down any ideas, experiences, or insights that you don't have room for in the main portion of the workbook. In addition, we suggest you invest in a blank notebook or journal to keep with you, so you'll be ready to record any lucky material you want to remember.

A Final Word...

As Gay pointed out in the preface, this workbook *will* make you lucky—*if* you use it. Your dedication, discipline, and persistence are the keys. As with anything you do, casual effort will yield casual results. The more diligent you are about using the workbook, the more luck you'll experience in your life.

We recommend you take your time going through each chapter. Set your intention to experience the deepest level of commitment, release, learning, and growth possible. Luck is available in every moment, everywhere. This workbook is designed to help you tune into it and live it.

And finally, remember, there is no perfect way to do the activities in this workbook or to fill in your journal and tracker. If you miss a day journaling or tracking, don't get upset or beat yourself up. Just pick up where you left off and continue. Give yourself the gift of a lucky life by sticking with your practice, no matter what. Rome wasn't built in a day, but over time, it *was* built.

Let's begin.

PART 2

Deepening Your Experience of the Eight Secrets

1

THE FIRST SECRET

Commit to Be a VLP—Very Lucky Person

As you learned in *Conscious Luck*, your commitments—both conscious and unconscious—have tremendous power. They've created the life you have right now. This is why *you change your luck the moment you make a conscious commitment to being lucky.* Without a conscious commitment, your unconscious commitments will likely hold you back.

Committing to luck opens the door, allowing you to step through and then, with the help of the rest of the Secrets, become luckier and luckier. **NOTE: If you want to turbocharge that process, please start using the 21-Day Luck Activation Journal found in Part 3 NOW.**

To strengthen your commitment to luck, remember an occasion when you were lucky and then anchor that feeling inside. This will serve as your touchstone going forward. The following journaling will help you do this.

Take a Moment to Reflect: Looking back over the course of your life, come up with 2 – 5 examples of when you've been lucky and write them here:

____

____

____

____

____

____

Can you see that you've been lucky in your life at least once?

In the unlikely event that you couldn't recall any examples of being lucky in your life, remind yourself of this undeniable truth: *A hundred million sperm started on the journey to fertilize an egg, and I have the DNA of the lucky ONE that made it there successfully! So I definitely have something going for me!* Yeah, we know, kind of silly—but true! At the very least, you're lucky enough to be here and breathing.

Before moving on to the next exercise, be sure to consciously register the internal feeling of being lucky.

Exercise: Your Commitment to Being Lucky

Step 1. Willingness is the first step of conscious change. Are you willing to commit to being lucky? If so, as an outward sign of your willingness, circle the word 'yes' here: **YES**

If you're not willing yet, that's okay. Just save this book for when you are. Go to your calendar and set a reminder to return to this book a week or a month or a year from now to check your willingness to commit to being lucky.

Step 2. Now, write out your commitment. Don't worry about whether you believe it or not, just write this sentence, (filling in your name) on the lines below: I, ____________, make a sincere commitment to being lucky, now and forever.

____

____

____

Take a Moment to Reflect: Writing this commitment can "activate" your specific barriers to being lucky/successful/happy. What did it bring up for you?

Examples:

- This is too easy.
- This is dumb.
- How can this work?
- Do I deserve to be lucky?
- Success requires hard work—not luck.

Don't get caught up in your reactions. In the space below, just write down any thoughts or feelings that came up. You can explore them further when we work with the second Secret.

____

____

____

____

____

____

Exercise: Imprinting Your Commitment on Your Conscious and Subconscious Mind

In this section, you're going to do an exercise you'll recognize from *Conscious Luck:* writing your commitment to being lucky using both your dominant and non-dominant hands.

We're asking you to repeat this exercise, which activates both sides of your brain and your subconscious mind, because of its remarkable power to establish luck at the core of your being. In fact, we recommend you repeat this exercise as often as possible—especially at the beginning of your Conscious Luck journey.

Step 1. Start by writing your commitment sentence again, using your dominant hand, which is the hand you always write with. (In other words, if you're right-handed, write the sentence with your right hand.)

Filling in your name, write this sentence on the lines below: I, __________, make a sincere commitment to being lucky, now and forever.

____

____

Step 2. Now, you're going to switch the pen or pencil to your nondominant hand and write the sentence again. Writing with your nondominant hand allows you more access to your subconscious mind. It also activates the half of your brain that isn't normally engaged when using your dominant hand, stimulating whole-brain thinking and more creativity.

Just scrawl out the sentence as best you can in the space below. It doesn't have to be legible to anybody but you.

I, __________, make a sincere commitment to being lucky, now and forever.

Step 3. Now, switch back to your dominant hand and write your commitment sentence again here:

____

____

____

Step 4. Then, write it once more with your nondominant hand here:

Don't go further until you've written your sentences exactly as asked. If you've done it correctly, you should have two sentences written with your dominant hand and two written with your nondominant hand.

When you finish, take a break. Go for a walk, perhaps, or get a bite to eat. Take your mind off this process for at least a few minutes. It needs some time to sink in.

When you come back from your break, you can go on to the next section or save it for another day. Whatever feels right to you.

Your Current Commitments

As mentioned earlier, it's your conscious and unconscious commitments that have created the life—and the luck—you have today. You may not like all that you've created, but it's important to remember your power: if you can create your life one way, you can create it another way.

However, if you haven't examined your commitments thoroughly, especially your unconscious ones, it can be hard to make positive changes no matter how much you want to. In fact, it's your unconscious commitments that often give rise to the chronic challenges you face in your life.

Here are some examples of **negative, unhelpful unconscious commitments**:

- Always playing it safe
- Being unhappy with my body
- Creating chaos and conflict in my relationships
- Being poor and "less than"
- Not completing things

These commitments lead to negative outcomes, such as not following your passions, being overweight or underweight., having unhappy relationships or not having a relationship at all, never having enough money, or failing to follow through in life.

We usually have **positive unconscious commitments** as well—typically instilled in childhood. Here are a few examples:

- Always doing my best
- Being considerate of others
- Giving back to my family and the community
- Being kind to animals
- Being courteous

These commitments form your character and values and help you succeed in life. Our **conscious commitments** are easier to identify. Here are a few examples:

- Exercising
- Eating well
- Being faithful to my partner
- Meditating regularly
- Attending religious services

Unfortunately, your negative unconscious commitments often undermine your ability to practice your conscious commitments. That's why it's so important to become aware of your negative unconscious commitments, and to understand how they influence your choices and behaviors.

Exercise: What Have You Been Committed to Up Until Now?

Step 1. Write down as many commitments as you can identify, both conscious and unconscious, positive and negative, in the space below. (For clues to your negative unconscious commitments, look at any bad habits, addictive behaviors, and areas of challenge you have.)

Step 2. You have the power to choose—at any moment—to create new *conscious* commitments. Take a moment to study the answers you just wrote. Are there any new commitments you'd like to make now? Here are a few examples:

- Being at my ideal weight
- Experiencing financial abundance
- Having a rewarding relationship
- Having a satisfying livelihood
- Acting on opportunities
- Being willing to reach out to new people

Write your new conscious commitments here:

____

____

____

____

____

____

____

____

____

____

In the next chapter, we'll explore how to stop unconscious commitments (in the form of limiting beliefs and negative mental conditioning) from sabotaging your progress toward more and more luck.

Harness the Power Of "Wanting"

At this point, you're *willing* to be lucky, you've *committed* to being lucky, and you've *examined your present commitments*, both conscious and unconscious. Perhaps you've adopted some new conscious commitments as well. Now it's time to harness the emotional power of *wanting* to be lucky.

Some spiritual traditions teach that "wanting," or having desires is wrong, or at least counterproductive, because it focuses your attention on what you lack. We don't agree. We believe that wanting and having desires are normal, natural human experiences. Everyone wants water, food, and shelter, as well as companionship, love, and abundance—and this wanting fuels our motivation to act. Let's take a moment right now to get in touch with the feeling of wanting something.

Exercise: What Does it Feel Like to Want Something?

Step 1. Close your eyes and feel what it's like to be just a little thirsty. Place your attention on your mouth and your throat, then imagine how lovely it would feel to drink some cool water. Let yourself want that water, and then imagine the cool liquid filling your mouth and slipping down your throat. Can you feel the sensation of thirst as well as the quenching of that thirst? When you feel complete, open your eyes.

Now let's take the next step—a step that will help you deepen and own your heart's desire to be lucky.

Step 2. Write the following sentence three times: I, __________, WANT to be lucky.

____

____

____

Step 3. Now close your eyes, place your hand over your heart and experience the desire to be lucky for a few seconds. Then shift to the feeling of already *being* lucky you anchored earlier in the chapter. Let the feeling of being lucky deepen and expand, radiating to all parts of your body as you take a few long, slow, deep belly-breaths. When you feel ready, open your eyes.

Take a Moment to Reflect: How did it feel to let yourself want something? In the space below, write down any insights or experiences you had while doing this exercise:

____

____

____

____

____

____

____

Exercise: Go Public with Your Commitment

Telling other people about your commitment to be lucky takes that commitment to a different level and gives it more power.

Step 1. Pick three people you'd like to share your commitment with. Look through your phone contacts or mentally review your circle of friends and family and see if anyone jumps out at you. If not, just pick people you think would be supportive. Write down the names you've selected below:

I'll share my commitment with: (Name)	How (phone, Zoom, in person):
______________________	______________________
______________________	______________________
______________________	______________________

Step 2. Take time to consider what you're going to say. You can simply tell them you've read a book about luck and have decided you're going to be "one of the lucky ones." Or you can be more formal about it and say something like, "I'm committing to creating luck and abundance for myself from now on, and I'm telling a few of my friends and family about it." Say whatever feels right to you.

Remember, this is not about getting their permission or approval or even their acknowledgement. It is simply you declaring your commitment to being lucky out loud, to the universe. The people you tell are just witnesses.

In truth, how your witnesses react to your statement isn't important. They may be supportive, but they may not. Sharing significant commitments about your life goals with someone can trigger that person's insecurities about their own life and priorities. If they react poorly, just give an inner shrug, smile, and thank them. It's likely they haven't done all the work you've done to claim your luck. Then, as soon as you can, recommit to being lucky by repeating your commitment to yourself three times.

Step 3. Once you have completed sharing your commitment, return to this page and journal any thoughts or insights you gleaned from your experience:

____

____

____

____

Acknowledge and Celebrate Yourself

Whenever you take action to make your life better, it's important to acknowledge and celebrate yourself! This is especially true when it requires some courage or discipline to take that action. To celebrate the work you've done so far, take a few minutes now to do "the happy dance," whatever that means for you. The more physical the action, the more it anchors your success.

Here are a few suggestions:

- Put on some music and dance
- Play your favorite song and sing along "loud and proud"
- High five yourself by clapping your hands together above your head and then pumping both fists into the air as you say, "YES!"
- Give yourself a scalp or shoulder massage
- Put your favorite beverage in a beautiful glass and raise it in a toast to yourself before you drink it
- Take a few minutes to play with your pet
- Find a friend and ask for a hug

Do whatever feels meaningful and enjoyable to you!

Commitment Requires Recommitment - Daily Practice

The thing about commitment is that it's not a one-and-done phenomenon. If you're human, there are going to be times when your old unconscious commitments reappear and throw you off track. Don't give yourself a hard time when this happens, even if it happens a lot; it's completely normal. Just use it as a cue to course correct by recommitting to your goals.

In the context of Conscious Luck, that means recommitting to being lucky. So whenever you're feeling unlucky, recommit to luck in writing, or simply take a few deep belly-breaths and say to yourself several times: I, __________, make a sincere commitment to being lucky, now and forever.

You can write the sentence below whenever you need to recommit.

____

____

____

If you've already begun using the 21-Day Activation Journal found in Part 3 of this workbook—and we hope you have—you're already writing your Conscious Luck commitment every day and listening to the Conscious Luck Activation Meditations in the morning and evening. This will help establish your commitment on a deeper level and accelerate your embrace of being a VLP—Very Lucky Person.

If you haven't done so, please go to www.consciousluck.com/workbook to download the morning and evening meditations that accompany the *Conscious Luck* book.

♣

Your commitment to being lucky is *the* crucial first step to experiencing more luck in your life, *but it's not enough all by itself.* Living a life of Conscious Luck requires additional core shifts and then daily practices, which is why there are seven more secrets left to explore.

Our next task is to clear any blocks and barriers we have that can sabotage our commitment to being lucky now and forever. Let's move on to Chapter 2.

2

THE SECOND SECRET

Release Your Personal Barriers to Good Fortune

The biggest barrier you face to being luckier is the negative mental conditioning you've unconsciously accumulated throughout your life. Even as you release your conditioning, your old default mental patterns and limiting beliefs often beckon that newly-awakened part of your mind to go back to sleep, in the "safe" confines of your familiar (and less lucky) habits of thinking.

That's why for luck to take root and grow, it's vitally important that you become aware of your outdated mental conditioning, let it go, and rewire your mind for luck through your new commitments. This is an ongoing process—one that requires you to be gentle and kind with yourself along the way.

The process also requires patience. There are many layers to your mental conditioning, much like a parfait (though not always a very delicious one). As you identify and heal one layer, other layers underneath it will surface and present themselves to you for release. As you successfully process each layer, more and more good fortune becomes possible for you.

The goal in this chapter is to release your personal barriers to luck *and to keep moving*. If you find yourself getting stuck here, give yourself permission to be satisfied with whatever release you receive from doing this chapter's exercises and journaling *once or twice*, and then move on to the third Secret. You can always come back and do the exercises and journaling for the second Secret again. In fact, we strongly recommend that you come back to the second Secret *anytime* you become aware of an old limiting belief or mental pattern you're ready to release.

You'll find your experiences with these exercises change as *you* change. And we predict you'll get different, deeper results each time you go through them.

So, let's get started.

The Four Luck-Limiting Beliefs

Your negative mental conditioning consists mostly of your limiting beliefs: core convictions you hold that limit not only what you think is possible for yourself, but also how much abundance you'll allow into your life.

In the context of luck, there are four major categories of limiting beliefs:

LIMITING BELIEF #1: I'm an unlucky person.

All of us face challenges, but those who self-identify as unlucky *expect* failure, bad luck, and difficulty. If you have this limiting belief, it's usually because misfortune in the past has soured your view of the future. This often creates a self-fulfilling prophecy.

Statements that exemplify unlucky thinking include:

- Nothing good ever happens for me.
- I never win anything.
- Things don't go my way.
- Life is a struggle.
- I'm the poster child for Murphy's Law.
- That's just my luck…

LIMITING BELIEF #2: I'm unworthy of luck.

Variations on this include: I'm not okay; I'm not good enough; I don't deserve to be lucky.

The feeling of unworthiness usually stems from one of two causes:

- **Self-Judgment: Past events and situations, usually from childhood, that you've misinterpreted to mean something negative about you that wasn't intended.**

You misconstrued events or things other people said or did, and made decisions about yourself based on them. For example, if your parents divorced—though it had nothing to do with you—you became convinced you'd somehow caused the split and decided you were "bad" or unlovable.

Another example would be that someone made an innocent comment or offered well-intentioned constructive criticism about your performance or behavior, but you took this as a global judgment about your abilities and worth. (I can't sing, I'm stupid, I'll never be good at anything athletic, I'm hopeless at school…)

- **"Curses": Intentionally hurtful messages from others that you've taken to heart and internalized.**

The second reason you can feel unworthy of luck is because someone "cursed" you. A curse is simply an intentionally negative message about your character or your abilities, expressed by people in your life—parents, teachers, other caregivers, siblings, former lovers, bullies, etc.—which you absorbed and accepted as true. Here are some examples:

- You'll never amount to anything.
- If you keep eating like that, you'll be as big as a house.
- You're so stupid.
- You were a mistake (an unplanned and unwanted child).
- For an adopted child: your real parents didn't want you.
- Bully messages: you're too fat, ugly, skinny, funny-looking…
- You're only a girl.
- You're a sissy boy, scaredy-cat…
- You're inferior…because of your skin color, your ethnicity, your religion, your nationality, your gender, your sexual orientation, any disability ("four-eyes", "cripple", "retard", and so on).

Hurtful messages like these live within you and become an everyday, always-on, background-noise fact of life that's so pervasive you often don't even realize it's there.

People say terrible things to one another all the time, but it doesn't always result in feeling cursed. The problem begins when you believe what is said to you or about you. Internalizing someone else's negative judgments about your lovability, value, appearance, potential, or any other aspect of you is what creates feelings of unworthiness that limit your luck.

LIMITING BELIEF #3: I come from an unlucky family

Variations on this include: Being unlucky is just in my genes; My parents, grandparents, or other relatives are (or have always been) unlucky.

Many people feel that they have "Inherited Bad Luck," and just like eye or hair color or height, being unlucky is just the way they were born, and it can't be changed.

Some examples:

- No one in my family goes to college.
- No one in my family has any money.
- No one in my family gets ahead.
- No one in my family owns a house.
- Everyone in my family is unhealthy, unhappy, poor, unlucky…
- Where I come from, my only choices are to end up dead or in jail.

If you have this limiting belief, it can lead to a fear of being lucky because 1) being lucky will make you different from your family and not belong, and 2) you don't want to "outshine" your family members with your good luck. More about this dynamic later in the chapter.

LIMITING BELIEF #4: I'm *afraid* of being lucky.

Variations on this include: If I'm lucky, bad things will happen to me; I don't feel comfortable being lucky; I feel guilty that others aren't lucky.

This fear surfaces and intensifies when you start to make good progress in life. As a result, you begin to sabotage your own success in some way, effectively torpedoing your luck.

This is what's known as an "Upper Limit Problem," and it's discussed at length in Gay's book, *The Big Leap*. We'll share more about how this problem specifically affects our luck later in this chapter.

The Art and Practice of Letting Go of Old Beliefs and Patterns

The first step in releasing your barriers to luck is *identifying* your unlucky mental conditioning—those beliefs and feelings that are running the show without your permission. Gaining awareness of what holds us back is the most important step in increasing our "luck-ability."

NOTE: As you become aware of your mental and emotional patterns, we suggest you simply *be* with them for a time—observing where you feel them in your body—rather than resisting and condemning them. There is truth to the old adage, *what you resist, persists*, so be very gentle here. The journaling exercises below will guide you to increased awareness of your barriers, and the techniques that follow will help you move beyond these "unlucky anchors" in order to create luck consciously.

Getting Clear on Your Limiting Beliefs—
Make the Unconscious Conscious

Journaling Exercise 1: Let's start with the first luck-limiting belief: *I'm an unlucky person.*

Take a Moment to Reflect: Take a deep, centering belly-breath and then, connecting within, think of the areas in your life in which you feel unlucky: money, relationships, work, children, health, appearance, or any other area that comes up for you. There might also be a specific period of time in your life when you felt unlucky.

Write down whatever comes up for you here:

____

____

____

____

EXTRA CREDIT: Writing with your nondominant hand automatically puts you in the realm of the subconscious and thus, the unknown. On a separate piece of paper, repeat the last journal exercise, this time writing with your non-dominant hand. No one will see what you write but you. See if anything new surfaces. If nothing comes up, that's fine.

Journaling Exercise 2: Next, we'll address the second luck-limiting belief: *I'm unworthy of luck.* There are two possible reasons for someone to feel unworthy of luck.

Reason 1: Self-Judgment about actions you've taken in your own life or as a result of misinterpreting past situations and comments from others.

Take a Moment to Reflect: Again, take a couple slow, centering belly-breaths and, connecting within, tune into your deepest feelings about yourself. Can you discover any reasons you may feel unworthy of luck, or any decisions you've made about whether you deserve to be lucky?

Continuing to take slow belly-breaths, consider any aspects of yourself that you condemn or judge harshly and any area of your life where you feel stuck. Where do you feel you are "not enough" or "not okay"? For example: I'm lazy, I'm undisciplined, I'm unattractive, I'm selfish, I'm indecisive...

Don't get caught up in any emotional reactions you may have to anything you find; simply keep breathing through the process and write whatever you uncover below:

Reason 2: Feeling Cursed due to internalizing intentionally hurtful comments from others.

Take a Moment to Reflect: Where have you felt cursed? And why? Who cursed you? Have you ever been told you were a family embarrassment, a black sheep, or you weren't going to amount to much?

Some possible areas in which you may feel cursed are:

- Love/relationships
- Money
- Health
- Appearance
- Not being wanted/lack of familial love
- Your gender
- Your weight
- Lack of education
- Your potential to achieve success

Investigate these questions to bring the awareness of any curses to the surface. Once the curses have surfaced, they can be cleared. Write whatever you discover here:

____

____

____

____

____

____

____

____

____

____

____

Let's get specific. Please fill in the lines on the left-hand side below with the curses you journaled about earlier. For this purpose, you can give these curses short one- or two-word names that have meaning for you.

On the right-hand side, write down the names of the people who cursed you. This isn't about blame or judgment of anyone. You're merely identifying the source of the curse so you can pull it out by its roots and fully release it.

Curse:	Who said it:
____________________	____________________
____________________	____________________
____________________	____________________
____________________	____________________
____________________	____________________
____________________	____________________
____________________	____________________
____________________	____________________
____________________	____________________
____________________	____________________

EXTRA CREDIT: **Writing with your nondominant hand.** On a separate piece of paper, do the two journaling exercises you just completed (about feeling unworthy of luck) AGAIN, this time writing with your nondominant hand. You don't have to show anyone what you wrote. It's very possible new insights will surface as you tap into your subconscious mind. If nothing comes up, that's fine.

NOTE: We suggest you try this technique of journaling using your nondominant hand whenever you want to give your subconscious a chance to express itself. Some limiting beliefs can be lodged very deeply and require repeated attention to be fully processed.

Now that you've identified your limiting beliefs and their sources, let's take the next step.

Separating from the "Unlucky Part of You"

It's time to activate and reinstate your own personal power, and to leave in the past the outdated version of you that's been in charge, wreaking havoc and holding you back from experiencing more luck and freedom in your life.

From *Conscious Luck*: "*There's a part of you that you've never fully examined, and it's keeping you from being fully lucky.* If you'll explore that aspect of yourself—just focus on it now in a special way—it will release its grip on you."

The following two exercises help you release 1) the first luck-limiting belief: your identification with your history of being unlucky, and 2) the third luck-limiting belief: "I come from an unlucky family," by creating "space" between you and your past experiences and relationships.

If you did these two exercises while reading *Conscious Luck*, please do them again. Repeating the exercises dramatically increases their effectiveness. Plus, you'll be building on them later in the chapter.

Exercise: The Luck Timeline

Step 1: Choose a curse or limiting belief from the previous exercises. (We encourage you to repeat this exercise with each of the curses and limiting beliefs you've identified.)

Step 2: Look at the list of time periods below and tune into the first time you were aware of feeling unlucky in the particular way you've chosen to examine—then point to that time on the Timeline. For example, if you've always felt unlucky, point to "Before I was born." If your feeling of unluckiness started in junior high or middle school, point to that line. There's no way to know for sure, of course, but just accept whatever answers you get from inside yourself:

After I finished going to school

When I was in college

When I was in high school

When I was in junior high or middle school

When I was in elementary school

Before I was in school

Before I could walk

Before I was born

Step 3: While pointing at the timeline with one hand, say the following phrase out loud: "**That was then.**" And then touch your chest with the palm of *your other hand* as you say, "**This is now.**"

You may feel resistance to doing this. Thoughts may come up like, *This is stupid* or *This will never work.* For now, just follow along. Do this exercise **at least ten times** saying, "**That was then**" as you point at the timeline, then touching your chest with the palm of *your other hand* as you say, "**This is now.**" Be sure to use both your hands—one to point at the timeline, and the other to touch your chest.

It's very important to repeat these phrases loudly at least ten or more times.

When complete, write down any observations you have from doing this exercise:

____

____

____

____

____

____

To get the most from this process, we recommend you repeat it often—especially in the early stages of your Conscious Luck journey. Each time you consciously separate yourself from any unlucky "baggage" from the past, you free yourself to intentionally create good fortune in all areas of your life.

Exercise: Breaking the Grip of the Past

This exercise specifically addresses the third limiting belief: "I've inherited my bad luck from my family or lineage, or from others who've had a strong influence on me."

Step 1. Think for a moment about who in your life has been unlucky. Most of us who feel unlucky have had family members such as parents or grandparents, siblings, former spouses or partners, or children who have felt unlucky too.

If there are significant people in your life (past or present) other than your parents or grandparents who you think have felt (or still feel) unlucky, write their names on the blank lines below. Use one line for each name.

Step 2. Take a minute to feel the energy of your parents, your grandparents, and any of the other people whose names you wrote down. Then, looking at the lines below, use your finger to point to "my parents," "my grandparents," or any other names you wrote, if you believe they felt (or still feel) unlucky. (If it was just one of your parents or grandparents, that's okay, still point to that line.)

If you didn't write down any names on the lines below and neither your parents nor your grandparents felt (or still feel) unlucky, that's fine; don't point. Skip Step 3 and move directly on to Step 4, the observations journaling below.

MY PARENTS

MY GRANDPARENTS

____

____

____

____

Step 3. Now, while thinking about your parents, grandparents, or other family members who have felt unlucky, use your finger to point to the appropriate line as you say, "**That was them**," or "**That was him/her,**" and then touch your chest with the palm of *your other hand* as you say, "**This is me.**" **Do this at least ten times.**

Step 4. When complete, write down any observations you made during this exercise.

For example, it could be that when you examined this belief of inherited bad luck more deeply, you found that your parents, grandparents, or the others you wrote down, didn't feel unlucky after all.

Or you might see that you've been *surrounded* by unlucky people and that they've influenced you more than you realized.

If you began the exercise knowing that you had no unlucky people around you, how did *that* feel?

Whatever your experience, capture your thoughts and feelings about it below:

____

____

____

____

____

____

After you finish doing this, take a break. We suggest you drink a glass of water and wash your hands to clear any old energy around you from this exercise. Another great idea is to take a walk outside and, if possible, go barefoot on grass, earth, or sand. Or use any other means you've found that helps ground you. Then, come back later or another day for the next exercise.

Fear of Luck or the Upper Limit Problem

As mentioned earlier, the fourth limiting belief, "I'm afraid of being lucky," or its variations: "If I'm lucky, bad things will happen," or "I'm not comfortable being lucky," are all closely associated with the Upper Limit Problem, or ULP (pronounced like "gulp" without the "g") discussed in Gay's book, *The Big Leap*. This particular type of ULP holds us back and makes us self-sabotage in ways that prevent us from creating and sustaining luck.

The technique to release a Luck ULP and stop sabotaging your good fortune has four steps:

1. Learn to recognize the ULP symptoms in yourself
2. Become aware of the fear underneath the symptoms
3. Gently let the fear go
4. Recommit to luck

Step 1: Do you have any symptoms of an ULP?

The symptoms of an ULP (related to Luck or anything else) can occur anytime you exceed the level of joy, love, success, luck, or wealth you think you deserve. We don't experience these symptoms on purpose. They are unconscious attempts to sabotage our positive momentum.

Here are some examples of possible ULP symptoms:

- Worrying (Anytime you're worrying and/or obsessing about something you have no control over, you're probably dealing with an ULP)
- Dwelling on past misfortune
- Feeling off-center in your body
- Getting sick or hurt soon after a positive event in your life
- Bickering or serious arguing with family or a significant other
- Criticizing or blaming yourself or others
- Deflecting compliments or praise
- Unexplained crying
- Messing up at work or in life immediately after having a significant win

Take a Moment to Reflect: Look again at the symptoms outlined above. **Do you experience one or more of these?** Are there any other symptoms, not included on the list, that you tend to experience when you find yourself feeling too happy, lucky, successful, or loved—that is to say, when life starts going well for you?

List below all the ULP symptoms you experience and then write any thoughts or feelings that come up in relation to them:

____

____

____

____

____

____

Your awareness of your ULP symptoms is an important element in overcoming the fourth limiting belief. You make a big leap forward in your ability to be lucky every time you "catch yourself" in the midst of an ULP symptom. The next step is to uncover the fear that underlies the symptom.

Step 2: Become aware of the fear underneath the ULP symptoms

There are three primary fears that can hold the Luck ULP in place:

1. I am afraid that if I'm lucky, I will be disloyal to my roots and leave people from my past behind. ___
2. I am afraid that if I'm lucky, more luck will bring more burdens. ___
3. I am afraid that if I'm lucky I will outshine _______ and make that person look or feel bad. ___

There are several impactful permutations of these fears, including:

- I am afraid that if I'm lucky others will be jealous. ___
- I am afraid that if I'm lucky, I'll feel guilty because others aren't. ___
- I'm afraid that if I'm lucky, I'll become a target for others' negativity. ___
- I'm afraid that if I'm lucky, my life will change, and I won't like it. ___
- Can I really be lucky now that my spouse or loved one has passed away? ___

Exercise: Identifying Your Fears

Which of the statements about fear resonate most with you? Look at them again and, just to the right of each sentence, rate on a scale of 1–10 how often you feel those fears: 1 for "never," 3 for "rarely," 5 for "sometimes," 7 for "often," and 10 for "all the time."

Take a Moment to Reflect: For the fears that you rated above a 5, take a moment to think of the ways this fear may have impacted you. Jot down any insights or thoughts you want to remember here:

___

___

Step 3: Gently let the fear go.

Once you finish identifying and rating your fears, pick the fear you feel the most often, close your eyes and bring your awareness to your body. Feel where that fear is present in your body. Then open your eyes and point to the place on the following body diagram where the fear is located.

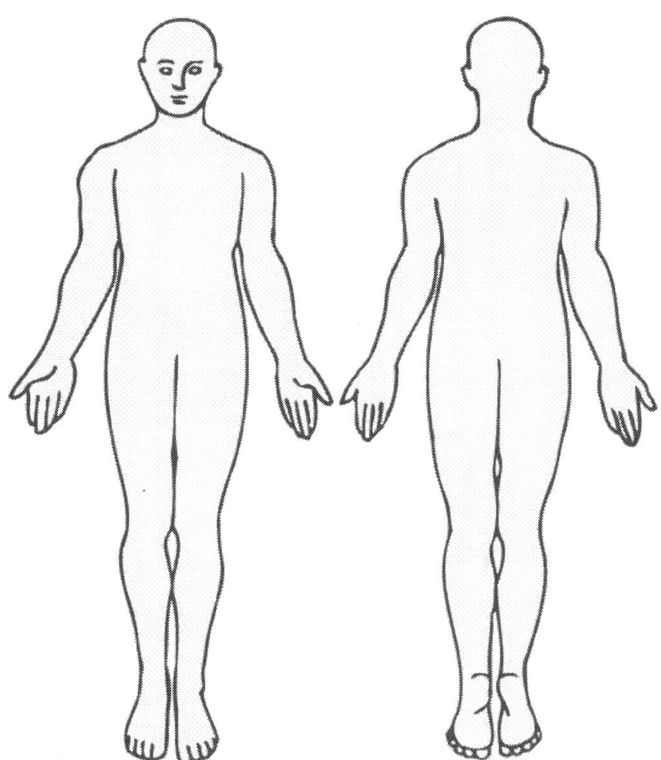

Now close your eyes once more, and again locate the places in your body where you feel the fear. Taking long, slow, deep breaths, just be with that feeling of fear until it dissipates. Don't try to get rid of it. Simply observe the feeling of fear and breathe into it. When you feel complete, take a few normal breaths, and then open your eyes.

If you didn't feel the feeling of fear dissipate significantly, don't worry. It may be lodged more deeply in your body. We'll address this in the next chapter about the third Secret. Simply continue with this exercise for now.

The next step is to repeat this exercise for all the fears described in the sentences in Step 2 that you rated as greater than a "5."

Remember, awareness is the most powerful healing tool available to move toward creating more luck in your life, but *it must be followed by action.* When you finish doing the exercise with all the symptoms and fears that you have time to address in any one session, end by **doing Step 4 immediately**.

Step 4: Recommit to Luck.

Every time you become aware of an ULP symptom and the fear beneath it, and then gently let go of that fear, it's important to consciously redirect your attention back to what you want, which is luck.

Return to your commitment to being lucky by saying or writing three times: I, ________ sincerely commit to being lucky, now and forever.

____

____

____

____

____

____

EXTRA CREDIT: On a separate piece of paper, write your three re-commitment sentences again, using your nondominant hand.

Take A Moment to Reflect: In the space below, journal any thoughts or insights that you had while working through this chapter that you want to capture.

____

____

____

____

____

____

You can see that the second secret of Conscious Luck requires a continual process of 1) letting go of anything that stops your forward progress, and then 2) recommitting to being lucky now and forever.

From now on, anytime you become aware of limiting beliefs, curses, inherited bad luck, ULP issues, and fears, simply return to this chapter and go through the exercises again. The releasing process gets easier and easier as you continue, and we promise you, any discomfort you feel along the way will be a small price to pay for the rising tide of good luck you'll experience as a result.

♣

Another significant personal barrier to luck that we'll be exploring more deeply is shame. In the next chapter, you'll learn not only how to release shame, but how to transform the space where shame "lives" in your body into a magnet for abundance.

3

THE THIRD SECRET

Transform Shame into a Magnet for Abundance

Being able to transform the energy of shame you hold in your body into a magnet for abundance and greater luck is a game-changer. It turns one of the most damaging and insidious problems you face in life into a powerful force for good. Yet, like many transformations, it may not be fully complete overnight.

In the previous chapter, we explained that overcoming your barriers to luck is not usually a linear process; you don't deal with a barrier once and never see it again. Growth occurs more in the shape of a spiral. A barrier may come up repeatedly, and each time it does, you address it again with an increasingly expansive version of yourself. And so it is with transforming shame.

In *Conscious Luck*, we defined guilt as feeling bad about *things you've done*, and shame as feeling bad about *who you are*. Though you may not consciously experience much shame in your life, most of us have it lodged somewhere in our bodies whether we're aware of it or not.

You can feel shame about almost anything: your appearance, your family, your level of education, having been in unhealthy or abusive relationships, something you did, or something that happened to you at a very young age—or at any age. You can even feel shame that isn't really yours but was passed down to you *in utero* or through your family lineage.

Sometimes it's difficult to recognize the feeling of shame. For many of us, shame is buried deep within, beneath negative feelings we're more familiar with, such as anger or sadness. This is because our negative emotions are layered, like that parfait we mentioned in Chapter 2. The layer closest to the surface is anger. Underneath anger is sadness, under sadness is fear, then guilt, and finally, shame.

Anger
Sadness
Fear
Guilt
Shame

As you work through the following exercises, if you can't identify a feeling of shame, that's okay. Try working with one of the other, more accessible emotions instead.

It's important not to get caught up in your feelings of shame (or any other emotion you access for this process), or in the events that caused the shame or other challenging emotion. In this process, you're dealing with your difficult emotions on the physiological level, rather than on the psychological level. Simply locate the feelings in the body.

In general, the negative emotions in the parfait follow a progression down the body. Anger is felt in the upper part of the body: we furrow our brows, flare our nostrils, clench our jaws, and experience tension in the back of our neck or between our shoulder blades. Sadness is usually experienced in the throat and chest areas, fear is often felt in the belly, and guilt and shame are often felt in the lower part of the body, in the pelvic area and down the legs.

Shame, however, has a unique quality, in that it can be felt almost anywhere in the body, depending on the events that instilled it initially. For example, if a person was slapped or spanked on the legs, buttocks, back, or hands, shame can be lodged in those parts of the body. Or, if someone was touched inappropriately in the genital region, the feeling of shame can be found there. If being humiliated by someone produced the shame, it can be experienced in the face, neck, or chest, like a blush. Wherever the sensation arises, place your focus there as you do the exercise.

As a reminder, we're not attempting to push away or resist any negative feelings that come up. Doing so will only keep them with us longer. Our intention is to be fully with our feelings, and to transform them into light.

You may think you've adequately processed your shame from the past through therapy or inner work, or through programs you've attended. We respect the work you've done, and still encourage you to do the next exercise, as it approaches the issue from a different angle and for a different purpose.

Whether you're new to shame work or you've done it many times, look at this process as an opportunity to go deeper, allowing you to gradually process all the layers and transform any residual hurt, anger, fear, shame, and guilt that still live in your body into light, which will magnetize luck and abundance to you.

Transforming Shame into Luck

The Conscious Luck Shame-Transforming process that follows is available at www.consciousluck.com/workbook as an audio file recorded in the authors' voices. Please listen to the recording in whichever voice you feel is most helpful.

Many people find it valuable to listen to the audio on a loop, as this provides an opportunity to stay in the settled state the exercise creates and repeat the process as many times as you want. Doing the exercise over and over again allows you to go deeper and deeper. You may even find that new images or memories surface. If this happens, just keep listening to the exercise and continue to bring light into your body until you feel complete.

If you're ready to transform shame or any other negative emotion into a magnet for more luck and abundance in your life, tune in to your preferred audio version and go through the shame-transforming process right now. We strongly recommend you listen to the audio of this process, but if you'd like to read the text of the exercise before or afterward to reinforce it, here it is:

The Conscious Luck Shame-Transforming Process

1. Start by closing your eyes, then taking a few deep belly-breaths and tuning into your body—the sensations you feel, your weight on the chair, bed, or floor. As you relax into awareness of your body, notice any feelings of shame present inside you. Don't get caught up in the emotional aspects or the reasons for your shame, simply do a scan of your body for any feelings of shame present.

Like the constant flow of thoughts in your mind, shame comes to you unbidden. You woke up one day, perhaps a lifetime ago, and it was there. You didn't have to ask for it. Perhaps you've felt burdened by it and have wanted it to disappear from your body, but that shame has remained with you anyway.

2. Take another deep belly-breath and gently focus on the presence of shame in various places in your body. For example, you might feel that it extends from your waist down through your legs: your buttocks, thighs, and calves. Part of that might be because, like many of us, that's where you were often struck physically while you were being shamed, or it might relate to feelings you have about your sexuality, or it might be about something else entirely.

   Perhaps you feel shame in your chest or stomach. Or in your hands or your face. It's not important whether you can feel it clearly right this moment or not. It might be below the surface of your conscious awareness. Even if you don't feel the physical sensation of shame at this moment, recall the general dimensions of it as you've felt it in the past.

   The physical component of shame needs to be at the forefront because that's your avenue to the psychological part of it.

3. Notice any tension, tingling, or other sensation in your body thoroughly and deeply. Let your attention rest on each area of sensation for about the length of three deep, easy belly-breaths, about twenty seconds, or until you feel some sort of a release—at least a little.

   If you don't get a release, it's usually because you're not willing to focus your attention on the shame long enough for it to release. Any troublesome feeling that you're willing to focus on and allow to exist will eventually transform into open space.

4. Now, imagine that open space—whatever its size—filling with light. You may experience this visually or as a felt sensation in your body. Let the

light pour into the spaces once occupied by shame like clear, sparkling water displacing muddy water in a glass.

Continue the process for another few breaths. Feel the physical sensation of shame anywhere you find it in your body until it releases into openness, then fill that space with light. Take a few minutes to savor the new experience of light, open space where there was constriction and heaviness before.

5. You were once rich in shame. It was like an inheritance. It came to you spontaneously, and absolutely free of charge. Shame once lit up areas of your body, and now those areas are being illuminated with something new and better. You've heard the saying "Like attracts like." Now, feel the truth of that saying in your body. A vast field of richness has opened inside you, and this inner richness attracts outer richness in the form of abundant money, health, purpose, and love. Breathe in this new richness, accept it, and let it make its home in your body.

6. The final step in this process is to infuse your being with the opposite of shame: self-love. To do this, bring to mind someone in your life whom you love deeply—a spouse, a child, a parent, a friend, or a pet. Feel the love in your heart for that special individual in your life. Let that feeling expand until it fills your internal space completely.

   Take another deep belly-breath and now switch your focus from your loved one to yourself. Don't let any thoughts about your faults or mistakes sidetrack you—keep your focus on your body. Just turn the stream of your love onto yourself, and let it flow, drenching you. Let the love soak in.

7. When you feel complete, take a few deep belly-breaths, and keeping your eyes closed, gradually start moving your body: wiggle your fingers and toes, do a gentle neck roll, stretch your arms and legs. Then when you're ready, open your eyes slowly. Take a little time to transition into your normal activity.

Take a Moment to Reflect: In the space below, write about any new insights or new feelings of freedom you have after doing the shame-transforming exercise.

Some possible areas to consider:

a. What are you aware of in your body now?
b. What's happening in your heart or in your mind?
c. Do you feel any new spaciousness or light in your body? Any emotional release or clearing? Any realizations or new understanding about your past?
d. How do you feel about yourself? Are you experiencing more self-love than before?

____

____

____

____

____

____

Over the next few days, you may notice your body adjusting to a new sense of freedom as your cells and memories reorient and the light you called in continues to transform the shame. Allow your body to adapt to your new normal.

If you'd like, take a few minutes two or three times a day (maybe in the morning before you get out of bed, at night before you go to sleep, and before or after lunch) to visualize the light that now fills those places in your body where you once felt shame. See this light extending out into the world in all directions, attracting more of what you want in your life directly to you.

NOTE: If there are places in your body where you still feel shame, please either repeat the same exercise again, or continue to the exercise that follows.

Exercise: Breaking the Grip of Shame in Your Body

The previous exercise may be all you need to transform any shame or other buried emotion in your body into a good-fortune-attracting magnet. However, if after some time doing the shame-transforming exercise you still feel residual shame, possibly from more deeply held stress or trauma, use the following exercise to deepen or complete the transformation process.

Step 1. Looking at the following image of the front and back of the body, point to a place where you still feel shame, anger, sadness, fear, or guilt—whichever emotion you've chosen to work with—in your own body.

Step 2. While pointing to the spot on the image, say the following phrase aloud: "**That was then.**" And then touch your chest with the palm of the *other hand* as you say, "**This is me, now.**" It is important to use this new phrase in its entirety, being sure to add the word "**now.**"

This is our opportunity to call ourselves into the present moment and own who we are *now*, letting go of whatever happened to cause shame in the past. Repeating this affirmation grounds you in the present and harnesses all the power, awareness, growth, and strength of the person you are today.

Do this exercise *at least ten times* saying, "**That was then**" as you point to the image of the body, then touching your chest with the palm of the other hand as you say, "**This is me, now.**"

Step 3. Either with your eyes closed or while looking at the image, imagine the part of your body that was affected by shame filling with light. You may experience this visually, or as a felt sensation in your body. Let the light expand from that place, filling every cell in your body and magnetizing luck to you.

Step 4. Take a few deep belly-breaths and savor being present with the physical sensation of light filling you from the top of your head to the soles of your feet.

If necessary, repeat the previous steps for each place in your body you still hold shame, fear, or other difficult emotions.

Step 5. Complete the exercise by taking three deep, slow belly-breaths and immediately do the journaling exercise that follows.

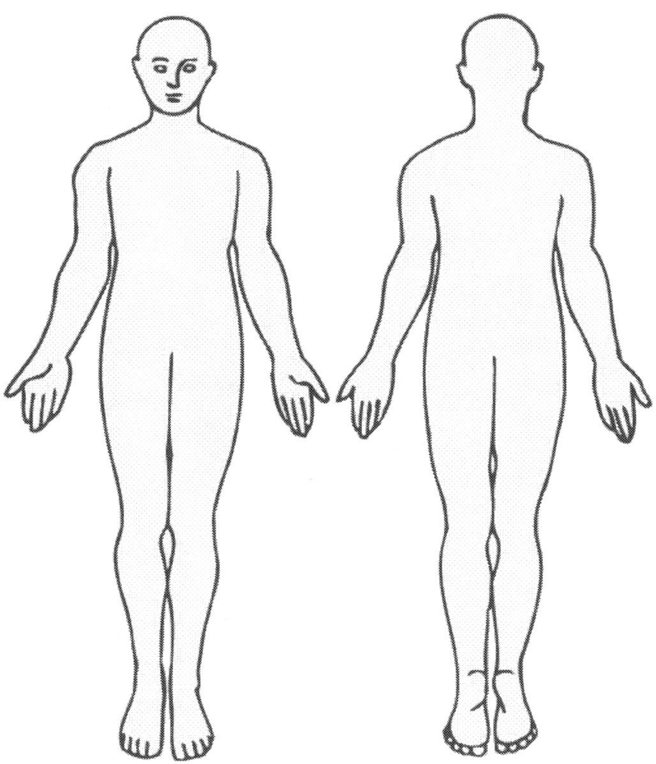

Take a Moment to Reflect: What do you feel in your body now? Some possible things to consider:

a. Do you feel the presence of light in your body?
b. Do you feel freer in your body?
c. Do you feel lighter, as in less heavy?
d. Is the energy in your body flowing more strongly?
e. How do you feel in your heart and mind?

Journal here to anchor the awareness of any new sense of freedom you now feel.

____

____

____

____

____

____

If there are still places in your body where you feel shame, please do either or both of the exercises again. Feel free to do them as often as you'd like—until you can no longer locate any shame in your body. We recommend doing these exercises if any feelings of shame return or if new ones arise.

Because of the layered, parfait-like arrangement of human emotions, each time you work through the exercise and experience some clearing, deeper freedom and more luck become available to you.

Out with the Old, In with the New

One of the benefits of doing the shame-transforming exercises is that as you feel less shame and other damaging emotions within yourself, you gain more energy to move forward in your life. Negative emotions stuck in your body can keep you stuck in your life. So as you clear your old, outdated emotions and replace them with light, you naturally have more access to the wellspring of positive energy within you, including your courage, creativity, joy, serenity, and love.

Take a Moment to Reflect: Take three slow and deep belly-breaths. Imagine breathing in energy and joy and breathing out peace and relaxation. Now, ask yourself the following questions:

1. Is there a past difficulty or obstacle I've struggled with that now feels more manageable?

2. Is there anything I've always wanted to do or try that I now feel I can move forward on?

In the space below, write any ideas that arise in response to these questions. (We'll explore the second question more deeply in the next chapter about the fourth Secret.)

Exercise: Anchoring Self-Love

A wonderful way to anchor your results from the self-love portion of the Transforming Shame into Luck exercise is to write the following statement to yourself three times:

I, __________, infuse myself with love. The light that illuminates my body is a magnet for abundance. I attract and enjoy wonderful luck, now and forever.

EXTRA CREDIT: **Writing with your nondominant hand.** On a separate piece of paper, repeat the self-love anchoring writing exercise you just did, this time using your nondominant hand. Allow this exercise to ground you in authentic self-love, and as a result, amplify your luck and abundance.

Now read the sentences you wrote aloud three times.
Breathe in this new declaration.
Choose it.
Own that it's yours.
And so it is.

A Final Word about "Parfait Diving"

Remember, getting to the bottom of your emotional parfait takes time. You dip in once, process whatever comes up, and then dip in again—this time a little deeper, perhaps accessing the next layer, where you'll likely find something new. You repeat these dips again and again until eventually you get to the bottom, down to your shame, which is one of the root causes of bad luck. It's extremely rare to make the dive all the way to the bottom in one trip.

That's why we encourage you to be patient with yourself and celebrate each step of progress. Think of clearing these personal barriers as an ongoing practice of continually discovering more and more about yourself as you transform the negative emotions you harbor into light-filled space, which is a magnet for abundance.

✤

With greater freedom, clarity of mind and heart, and creativity, we can consciously choose goals more in alignment with who we are and what we want more of in our lives. In the next chapter, you'll work on creating your goals in a way that attracts more luck *and* makes them easier to achieve.

4

THE FOURTH SECRET

Have Luck-Worthy Goals

In *Conscious Luck*, you learned a surprising formula: If you want to be luckier, have luck-worthy goals! Everyone, even those who feel extremely lucky, will find more success and abundance in life by adjusting their goals to attract luck—and giving luck plenty of good reasons to visit.

The goals we're talking about are not the items on your daily to-do list or the immediate demands you face at work or home, but the deeper aspirations you have about your contribution to the world, using your unique gifts and abilities, and living your best life.

Even so, by the end of this chapter, you'll learn how to "luckify" *any* goal, including those that are mundane and/or pressing, to add some luck-boosting power.

As you read in *Conscious Luck*, "luck chases worthy goals." Goals that inspire luck to chase after them meet three criteria:

- They're deeply meaningful to you.
- They light you up and allow you to do what you most love to do.
- They're beneficial to you personally *and* to other people.

Are Your Goals Luck-Worthy?

In the following pages, you'll be reviewing your goals to see if they satisfy the three requirements of luck-worthiness. And if they don't, you're going to learn how to luckify them. Let's start by writing some goals down.

Exercise: What Are Your Current Goals?

Step 1. Write down your current goals. If you don't have any goals at this time, please skip to the next exercise titled **Goals 101** to create some.

At this point, don't worry about whether your goals are luck-worthy or not. You also don't need to worry about whether they are goals you need to take care of immediately, goals you want to accomplish in the months ahead, or longer-term life goals. Just list as many goals as you'd like in the space below.

If you need more space, you can use the NOTES section at the back of the book. Feel free to transfer the goals you wrote down on page 65 of *Conscious Luck* as well.

Step 2. Now, look at the list that you just wrote and place an asterisk by the three goals that speak to you the most. Then write those three goals on the following lines using the format, "If I were lucky, I'd (fill in your goal)."

1.

____

2. ____

____

____

3. ____

____

____

If you were able to complete this section, great. Please skip the next exercise and go directly to the section titled, *Luck-Worthy Goal Requirement #1.*

Exercise: Goals 101

If you couldn't think of any specific goals you have, we recommend you take time now to discover at least three.

Step 1. To start, please answer the following question: "If I were totally, completely lucky, what would I be doing or what would I have that I'm not doing or don't have right now?"

For example:

- If I were lucky, I'd make a six-figure income doing something I enjoy.
- If I were lucky, I'd be fit and have a lot of energy.
- If I were lucky, I'd live in a house in the mountains with a view.
- If I were lucky, I'd pay off all my bills and still have money left to put in savings.
- If I were lucky, I'd have time to paint (or write, or dance, or sing, or…) every day.
- If I were lucky, I'd buy a new energy-efficient car with all cash.

Write your answers below using the "If I were lucky…" format. Write as many as you'd like.

Step 2. Next, review your answers and put an asterisk by the three that are most compelling to you, right now. Write those three below in the same "If I were lucky…" format.

My Current Goals:

1.

2.

3.

Now, let's do the Conscious Luck Sniff Test on your goals.

Luck-Worthy Goal Requirement #1. Your Goals Are Deeply Meaningful to You

It's important to have goals that mean something to you, because working toward a goal is like climbing a ladder to reach the top of a wall—you want to be sure the ladder is leaning against the right wall. Otherwise you could get to the top and realize that all your effort has taken you somewhere you don't really want to be.

Before we explore whether your goals meet this requirement, let's look at what's meaningful to you.

Take a Moment to Reflect: Ask yourself: ***What is meaningful to me? What do I* really *want in my life?***

If any of your current goals include having "more money" or "more time," we want you to go deeper to find what's underneath that. What will having more money or time give you or allow you to do? Your answers will tell you what's truly meaningful to you!

Here are some examples:

- Spend time with my family
- Have peace of mind about money
- Be able to donate to my church or other causes
- Be able to volunteer in my community
- Be able to pursue creative projects
- Have a substantial amount of savings put aside for emergencies
- Feed my family organic food
- Create wonderful memories with the people I love

Write your answers below:

____

____

____

If you feel stuck, or want to explore this from another angle, ask yourself this powerfully clarifying question: ***What breaks my heart in this world?***

Your answers will not only give you clues about what really matters to you, but might also suggest the social causes you'd find most rewarding to get involved in. Here are some examples:

- The plight of the homeless
- Cruelty to animals
- The loneliness epidemic among the elderly
- Racial injustice
- Vanishing wildlife habitats
- Childhood obesity
- Climate change
- Illiteracy

Write yours below:

We hope answering these questions has given you a better idea of what's meaningful to you. Now let's review your goals through that lens.

Exercise: How Are Your Goals Meaningful?

As you know, connecting your goals to what you find meaningful will amplify the luck-attracting quality of those goals. To do this, look at each of your current goals and, based on what you discovered in your journaling, ask yourself, "*How* is this goal meaningful to me?"

You may find these questions helpful:

- How will this goal bring me closer to what I really want?
- How will this goal help me fulfill my unique sense of purpose?
- If I reach this goal, in what ways will I experience a sense of deep satisfaction and meaning?

As an example, let's use one of the sample goals from the *What Are Your Current Goals?* exercise: "If I were lucky, I'd buy a new energy-efficient car with all cash." This goal is meaningful because:

1. It's in alignment with my commitment to be environmentally responsible.
2. By paying with all cash, I avoid taking on any additional debt.
3. The savings in fuel costs will allow me to take a trip to visit someone special, which I can't afford to do with my less fuel-efficient car.

Jot down how each of your goals is meaningful below:

Goal 1:

____

____

____

____

Goal 2:

Goal 3:

Take a Moment to Reflect: How does it feel to connect your goals with what's meaningful to you? Write what comes up for you in the space below:

Now that you've verified that your goals are meaningful, the next step is to determine if they light you up. If you feel that your goals aren't as meaningful as you'd like them to be, don't worry, later in the chapter you'll have a chance to tweak them.

Luck-Worthy Goal Requirement #2. **Your Goals Light You Up**

To find out whether a goal lights you up, you'll need to evaluate how you feel about that goal.

To start, ask yourself these questions about *each* of the three goals you listed as *My Current Goals* in Step 2 of the *What Are Your Current Goals?* exercise or the *Goals 101* exercise:

- Will achieving this goal allow me to do something I love to do?
- Do I get excited or feel eager about working toward this goal?
- If I didn't make a dime achieving this goal, would I still want to do it?

Jot down anything that comes up for you in the space below:

____

____

____

____

____

____

Your answers—coupled with the following meditation that allows you to check in directly with your heart—will let you know if the goals you wrote really do light you up.

Ask Your Heart

To see if your goals make your heart sing, download the Conscious Luck Heart Meditation, recorded in the authors' voices at www.consciousluck.com/workbook. Again, please choose the recording in the voice that works best for you.

We strongly recommend you listen to the recording to do this meditation. After you've done so, if you'd like to read the text of the meditation to reinforce its message, here it is:

The Conscious Luck Heart Meditation

1. To start, take a few minutes to review the goals you've written down.
2. Then, sit comfortably in a place where you won't be disturbed. Close your eyes and take three deep, slow belly-breaths.

3. Now, in your mind, not out loud, say the first goal on your list. Let the words drop into the stillness of your inner world like a stone into a pool, and feel the vibrations resonate in your body. Pay special attention to how these vibrations feel in your heart area.
4. Do you feel expansion or contraction in your chest? Do you feel like laughing? Do you feel excited? Bottom line, does your goal light you up? If not, that goal is not going to draw luck to you. Play around with the goal, adjusting it until it creates the whole-body smile we're going for. If you can't, put it aside and continue with the next goal on your list.
5. Repeat this process with all the goals you've written down. You can use all the goals you initially wrote in Step 1 of either the *My Current Goals* exercise or the *Goals 101* exercise, or just the three you selected in Step 2 of either exercise. If you test all your goals, you might find some on your initial list are more compelling than the ones you selected. This is good information to have. Note the ones that pass the test.
6. Now you're going to prioritize your goals using the same process. Keeping your eyes closed, go through each of your goals again, feeling the effect of that goal in your heart, and pay attention to which goal is the most expanding, the most exciting. When you accomplish your most exciting, heart-expanding goal, we suggest you repeat this part of the exercise at that time to determine the next goal your heart wants you to tackle.
7. When you feel complete, take another deep belly-breath or two and then open your eyes.

Take a Moment to Reflect: What came up for you during this process? Which goal came forward as the one to do first? How do you feel about that? Were you surprised by anything you discovered? Write your answers in the space below:

____

____

____

____

If one or more of your goals didn't light you up, that's okay. You may have committed to something that doesn't quite line up with who you are. Or you may have chosen something that was more of a "should" for you. Give yourself permission to switch the goal for another more inspiring one, if possible.

If for some reason you can't switch goals, there is another way forward. Ask yourself: *Does the goal contain elements I love and that light me up, which I can then lean into to complete it?*

Take a few minutes now to either choose another, more stirring goal from your initial list or find the things about your less-than-ideal goal that *do* light you up so that you can attract more luck as you follow through.

NOTE: If you do choose another goal, one that's more inspiring and exciting, make sure that your new goal meets the requirement of being meaningful before going on to Luck-Worthy Goal Requirement #3.

In the space below, capture your insights, thoughts, and feelings about how to proceed:

Whatever you uncovered through your work in this section—whether your goals are spot-on or need some adjusting to light you up—is extremely valuable. Later in the chapter, you'll be given the chance to incorporate what you learned here to create goals that are truly luck-worthy for you.

Luck-Worthy Goal Requirement #3. Your Goals Benefit You and Others

As you know, when your goals meet this luck-worthy requirement, it aligns you with the benevolent forces at work in the universe. In turn, those forces carry you along, helping you succeed through what we call "winks from the universe": synchronicities, unexpected support from others, breakthroughs, fortunate hunches, and other lucky breaks. Call it the "good karma" effect!

On the other hand, goals that only enrich you don't inspire support from those unseen forces—nor, understandably, from the people around you. What's worse, if a goal is achieved at the expense of others, it could even boomerang and come back to hurt you.

So, to keep the winds of luck at your back—pushing you toward your desired finish line—make sure your goals include some altruistic mojo.

Take a Moment to Reflect: Ask yourself these questions about *each* of the three goals you listed in Step 2 of either the *My Current Goals* exercise or the *Goals 101* exercise:

- Does the achievement of my goal help at least one other person—a family member, a friend, a client, someone in my community?
- Does my goal inspire compassion or kindness in me or others?
- Does my goal HARM anyone?

Write what comes up for you in the space below:

____

____

____

____

____

____

If your goals meet this requirement, that's terrific. Get ready for some winks from the universe and support from the people around you to help you accomplish what you're setting out to do. You can skip ahead to the Writing Your Goals *Again* section if you'd like.

If your goals didn't meet this requirement, continue to the next section.

Not All Altruism Is Obvious

If you don't see how your goals benefit others, it could help to look at them a little differently. The benefits may be indirect.

For example, say one of your goals is to get fit. Clearly, achieving that goal will benefit you, but the benefit could also extend to other people. Being more fit will likely make you:

- **A more positive person.** Being in better physical shape usually translates to better brain chemistry and more sustained well-being.

- **More fun to hang out with**. Having improved health, greater energy, and more vitality can make you more active and open to adventure.

- **More generous with your talents and abilities**. Fitness has been shown to increase one's confidence, which could lead to your being more open to sharing yourself more fully with the people around you.

Your turn. For *each* of your goals that don't meet this requirement, use this approach to find indirect benefits to others that might arise from achieving that goal. Ask yourself, *Is there any way this goal could benefit others?*

____

____

____

____

____

____

We hope you found some ways that your goals benefit others. If not, it doesn't mean you have to discard those goals; it just means you may not attract as much luck as you would with goals that include that altruistic element. If that's the case, we suggest you pay close attention to the section later in the chapter about adding acts of meaning, joy, and service to your life as an additional way to attract luck and reach your goals.

In the next exercise, you'll have a chance to take everything you've learned about yourself and your goals and do a bit of luck-worthy tweaking.

Writing Your Goals *Again*

You've probably heard the saying, *knowledge is power*. We believe it's *applied* knowledge that's power. In the exercise that follows, you'll have the chance to apply all the self-knowledge you've gained by doing the previous exercises and journaling, to create the most luck-worthy goals possible.

Exercise: Putting It All Together

Step 1. Go back to the *My Current Goals* or the *Goals 101* list at the beginning of this chapter and take a few minutes to review the three goals you wrote there.

Step 2. Next, review the insights you wrote down in each of the Luck-Worthy Goal Requirement sections.

Step 3. Incorporating all you've discovered so far, rewrite your goals to include as many of the luck-worthy elements as possible. Please use the "If I were lucky..." format. (If you don't need to rewrite your goals, skip to Step 4 and ask yourself all the questions that apply.)

____

____

____

____

____

____

Step 4. Take a deep breath and pause. Now, reread your goals. You might even want to read them aloud. Notice how you feel about them. Do these goals resonate deeply? Do they excite you? Can you see ways in which they benefit others? Were there any changes from the goals you wrote at the beginning of the chapter? Write down anything that comes up for you in the space below:

Step 5. Redo the Conscious Luck Heart Meditation for each of your three Luck-Worthy goals, focusing on Step 6 of the meditation. Afterward, place an asterisk by the goal that felt the most expanding and exciting.

Are Your Goals *Urgent* or *Important*?

As it turns out, not all goals are created equal. In Stephen Covey's book, *The Seven Habits of Highly Successful People*, he points out that many of us spend our lives taking care of the urgent demands we face daily, and over time, lose sight of the important long-term goals that would enable us to live our best lives. As a result, we may never get around to the things that are truly essential to us.

The work of noted psychologist Abraham Maslow—particularly his theory of the hierarchy of needs—gives us valuable insights into this widespread problem. According to Maslow, until our more basic survival needs of food, shelter, physical safety, and security are met, we can't focus on our higher needs: love, a sense of belonging, achievement, self-actualization, and spiritual aspirations. Your urgent goals usually involve your immediate survival needs, while your important longer-term goals bring you closer to living your full potential.

This is why it's vital to be aware of the difference between the two types of goals, and as much as possible, to keep the important ones on your radar.

Of course, there are times in life when postponing your long-term goals to "put out fires" or "put food on the table" is necessary. If, while going through this chapter, you've realized that you have current goals that are more pressing and short-term—for example, you need to make enough money to pay your rent, mortgage, or credit card balances next month, or your children need more of your attention than usual, or you have a relationship or health issue you need to address—don't be discouraged. It's possible to make urgent goals like these luck-worthy too!

If that isn't your situation at present, simply read through the following exercise. You can use the luckifying process on short-term projects or goals that may pop up in the future.

Exercise: How to Luckify an Urgent Goal

Let's say, for example, that your goal is to pay your rent this month and have money left over. You'd state your goal like this: If I were lucky, I'd be able to pay my rent and have money left over.

Step 1: Think about your urgent goals and select the one that you feel you most need to attend to. Write it below:

If I were lucky,

____

Step 2: Now luckify the goal you wrote down. That means identifying the three qualities in your goal that make it luck-worthy by asking yourself the following questions.

a. **How is it meaningful?**

Let's continue with our rent example: How is my goal of paying my rent and having money left over meaningful to me?

Knowing that your rent and important bills are paid can have a profound positive effect on your sense of well-being and integrity, which is certainly meaningful.

In addition, if you have money left over, what projects, initiatives, or higher-level growth experiences could you take on? Chances are, without the worry of your rent hanging over you, you'd have a lot more bandwidth and greater creativity to generate additional income and focus on your deeper, more meaningful aims in life.

How will accomplishing your goal be meaningful to you?

____

____

____

____

____

____

b. **Does it light me up? If so, how?**

Using the rent example again: Does paying my rent and having money left over light me up?

Here's a way to check this one out: Close your eyes and imagine your rent is paid in full—and you still have money left over. How does that feel? Are you happier? Lighter?

Once you determine that your goal lights you up, ask yourself *how* it lights you up. In our example: In what ways does paying my rent light me up?

Having the freedom from worry about paying your bills could light you up by giving you a renewed capacity to feel passionate and excited about pursuing some long-held goals—which previously may have seemed out of reach—and allowing you to cultivate your natural creativity, talents, and abilities.

Does accomplishing your urgent goal light you up? If so, how?

____

____

____

____

____

____

c. **How does it benefit me and others?**

In the paying rent example:

You and the others in your household will benefit by maintaining a roof over your heads and by reducing the general worry and tension that survival issues can generate.

In addition, the landlord and the landlord's family benefit, as well as any creditors the landlord pays. Paying the rent can have quite the ripple effect.

How will accomplishing your goal benefit you and others?

____

____

____

____

Having these perspectives about your urgent goals will transform the energy and mindset you have about them, enhancing your ability to attract luck—which will help you achieve them.

Adding Meaning, Joy, and Service along the Way

Here's a final tip for attracting luck as you work toward achieving your goals.

So far, we've explored how focusing on the meaningful, joyful, and altruistic aspects of your goals makes them luck-worthy. But there is another way to be a magnet for luck: **by including daily or weekly luck-attracting activities—unrelated to your goals—on your to-do list.**

To keep what's truly important to you from getting lost in the demands of daily life, make a commitment to schedule time each day, or at the very least each week, to do something, *in addition to working toward your goals*, that's meaningful to you, brings you joy, is of service to others—or all three! For example, volunteer to help someone learn to read, take a dance lesson, take a long nature hike with your dog, or participate in a local food drive.

Commit at least 15–20 minutes each day, or a few hours each week, to doing activities that align with your values and passions. This will create a strong foundation for your spirit to blossom—and your luck to grow.

Take a Moment to Reflect: Based on the insights you've gained in this chapter, in the space below, write down some of your personal luckifiers—activities that are meaningful to you, bring you joy, and are of service to others:

____

____

Refer to this list when using a daily planner or when filling out your 30-Day Tracker pages in Part 3 of this workbook.

Now it's time to take all the insights and self-understanding you've gained from your work in this chapter so far and apply them to working—a little every day—toward a luck-worthy goal. The next section will help you master the art of breaking bigger goals down into small doable steps.

Creating Next Steps for Your Goals

This section's exercise involves picking one goal to focus on for the next thirty days. You'll be tracking your progress toward your selected goal in the same 30-Day Tracker mentioned earlier.

You can do this exercise in one of two ways:

Option 1: Using the luck-worthy life goal you identified as your first priority in the *Putting It All Together* exercise, find a smaller sub-goal you could work on during the next 30-days to move that larger life goal forward.

OR

Option 2: Pick a more urgent goal that you want to complete in the next 30 days. It doesn't have to be related to your long-term life goals.

Once you decide, go to the exercise below for the option you selected.

Option 1 Exercise: Working with Your Luck-Worthy Life Goal

Step 1. If you decide to work with option 1, on the line below, write down the prioritized goal you put an asterisk by in the *Putting It All Together* exercise (found a few pages back in the section titled **Writing Your Goals *Again***).

MY GOAL: ______________________________

Step 2. Brainstorm smaller sub-goals that serve your larger goal, and which you can achieve in the next 30 days. (You'll break your chosen sub-goal into action steps later.)

For example: Say one of your luck-worthy life goals is to write a historical fiction novel, and this is the goal you select to use for this exercise. Ask yourself: *What can I do in the next 30 days to get closer to that goal?*

One answer might be to write a rough outline of your book, which becomes your 30-day sub-goal.

Your turn! In the space below, write some answers to the question: *What can I do in the next 30 days to get closer to the goal I selected?*

____

____

____

____

____

____

Step 3. Looking at the list of the possible 30-day sub-goals you just created, choose the one that feels best to you and put the number 1 by it.

Step 4. Write your selected sub-goal in a time-bound way. For example: By (date), I will have written an outline of my historical fiction novel.

MY 30-DAY SUB-GOAL:

____

____

This is your 30-Day goal. Now go directly to the **Brainstorming Action Steps** exercise that comes directly after the Option 2 exercise below.

Option 2 Exercise: Working with an Urgent Goal

Step 1. If you choose to work with option 2, pick an urgent goal to focus on for the next 30 days. If you haven't already done so, do the luckifying exercise (found a few pages back in the section titled **Are Your Goals Urgent or Important?**) for that goal to find the three elements that will attract luck and help you achieve it.

Write your urgent goal below. Here are some examples: paying my rent, helping my child prepare for the SAT next month, meeting an important work deadline, lowering my cholesterol or blood pressure for an upcoming insurance physical.

MY URGENT GOAL:

Step 2. You may or may not be able to complete that urgent goal within 30 days, but if not, you can certainly get closer. What can you do in the next 30 days to accomplish or get closer to your goal?

Let's return to the example of the urgent goal of paying the rent that we've already luckified earlier.

For this question, you'll first need to determine exactly how much more money you need to pay your rent. Or in other words, after calculating how much money you have and how much you need to pay toward all your other financial obligations, what's your shortfall on the rent? Let's say you're $300 short.

Next, you'll brainstorm ways to come up with that $300. For example:

- Clean out your garage, attic, and closets, and have a virtual "garage sale" on eBay, Etsy, Craigslist or Facebook Marketplace.
- Give up your most expensive nonessential spending habit for a month—Starbucks, wine, gourmet cheeses, etc.—and put that money toward your rent.
- Call a specific creditor and negotiate a more favorable payment program.
- Offer a talent or special skill you have for hire—cooking, writing,

gardening, organizing, decluttering, dog-walking, teaching music lessons or a foreign language.
- Create art or jewelry to sell.

In the space below, write some answers to the question: *What can I do in the next 30 days to accomplish or get closer to the urgent goal I selected?*

____

____

____

____

____

____

Step 3. Select one of your ideas to use as a 30-day goal and write it in a time-bound way.

For our rent example: By (date), I will make at least an extra $(amount) by organizing a virtual garage sale, and I'll use this sum to pay my rent.

MY 30-DAY GOAL:

____

____

Now that you've identified your 30-Day goal, you're ready to do the Brainstorming Action Steps exercise that follows.

Brainstorming Action Steps

The next step for both options 1 and 2 is to break down your 30-day goal into smaller, more bite-sized pieces known as action steps. An action step is the smallest complete action you can take in service to a project or goal. It's not too broad and, by definition, doesn't require multiple steps.

Option 1 Example:

For the goal of writing an outline for a historical novel, here are some examples of ideas for action steps:

- Take an online fiction writing course.
- Read a book about writing fiction.
- Join a fiction writers' group to start getting feedback from other writers.
- Research the time period to set the novel in.
- Write down ideas for plots and characters.
- Read the most critically acclaimed example of the genre.
- Schedule a daily 30-minute free-writing period.

Option 2 Example:

Continuing with our paying the rent example, here are some ideas for action steps to organize the virtual garage sale:

- Schedule time to go through your closets, jewelry box, attic, shed, basement, or storage unit to find things you don't use and can sell.
- Wash and iron any clothes you decide to sell.
- Clean, and, if necessary, repair any items you find to sell.
- Do some online research to determine fair prices for your sale items.
- Research if there are any collectors you can contact for items like baseball cards or Fiestaware® that might have more specialized market value.
- Take photos to post of all the items you're selling.
- Write descriptions of your items, and along with the photos, post them on the virtual venues you've selected.
- Research places to donate items that don't sell and that you don't want to keep.

Now it's your turn…

Step 1. In the space below, brainstorm ideas for action steps for your goal. Don't worry about whether an idea is possible or practical. You're just brainstorming—no commitment yet.

Be sure to bookmark this list, as you'll be coming back to it—adding to it or selecting your next task as you complete an action step.

Step 2. Reviewing the ideas you generated in Step 1, pick the ones that resonate with you and write those down here, one per line:

Step 3. Is there a "time order" in which to do the steps that makes the most sense? Do any of the steps build upon any others? On the list you just wrote, number your action steps in order of importance or sequence.

NOTE: When you begin using the 30-day Tracker in Part 3, you'll use the 30-day goal you selected and its accompanying action steps to complete the "The Luck-Worthy Goal or action step I am focusing on today is" section of the Tracker. You'll be slotting in the action steps as you go along.

If you've successfully completed all the exercises and journaling to this point, you've formulated between one and three goals that meet the Luck-Worthy Goal criteria, and one 30-day goal—either an urgent, short-term goal or a sub-goal of one of your larger life goals. You've also come up with a list of bite-sized action steps you can take to achieve your goal. In short, you've learned how to create a viable luck-attracting plan for your current goals, which you can use for all your future goals. Well done, you!

Goals Are Good

Whatever your attitude toward goals has been until now, we hope this chapter has increased your appreciation for their power. Goals help us harness our energy and attention to actually do the things we care about in life. They provide a target for us to aim at and a destination to go toward, day by fleeting day. Without goals, our progress would be haphazard, and almost certainly slower.

To top it off, when we realize that goals that are luck-worthy can help facilitate *their own achievement*, it makes us prize them even more.

For all these reasons, we recommend you make a commitment now to create luck-worthy goals for the rest of your life. We know you'll reap big rewards.

♣

Congratulations! You've completed the first four Secrets, which form the foundation for living a consciously lucky life.

In the next chapter, which is about taking bold action to increase your luck, you'll begin exploring the four Daily Living Secrets and applying them to your unique mind-body complex and circumstances—the same way you did in these first four chapters. Delving more deeply into the Secrets and then using them regularly in your daily life will make you a truly stellar luck-attractor.

But for now, take a few minutes to savor all you've accomplished so far, and celebrate you, your follow-through, and your willingness to do this deep work. Please visit the Conscious Luck Global Community group Facebook page and let us know that you completed the exercises and journaling for the Foundational Secrets and how that's affected your life. It will be inspiring for the whole community. Plus, we want to applaud your work and encourage you to keep going. The world needs more lucky people!

5

THE FIFTH SECRET

Take Bold Action Consistently

And now it's time to get this show on the road! In other words, to begin the hands-on, out-in-the-world part of your Conscious Luck journey.

The first four Conscious Luck Secrets emphasize internal shifts—committing to change, adjusting your beliefs, clearing your emotions, and aligning your vision for your life—as paths to greater luck. In this chapter we explore the first of the four daily practices, which are the nuts-and-bolts, active steps you can take every day to build a lucky life.

The fifth Conscious Luck Secret, Take Bold Action Consistently, might sound daunting, but all it really means is making an effort on a regular basis to get out of your comfort zone. You can do this by trying something new, being more spontaneous, taking risks, and asking for what you want.

Mix It Up a Little

As you learned in *Conscious Luck*, one of the easiest ways to try something new is to simply change up your routines. You can do this by varying your walking or driving routes, brushing your teeth or your hair with the hand you don't usually use, visiting unfamiliar stores, trying out new styles and colors of clothing, getting a new hairdo, or experimenting with various cuisines.

Changing your familiar patterns stimulates different areas of your brain and exposes you to new people, places, and possibilities, which can take you in new—luckier—directions. What would mixing it up look like for you?

Exercise: Making Your Mix-It-Up List

Step 1. Take a moment to think of your current daily routines. Here are some questions to get you started:

- What time do you get up?
- Which side of the bed do you sleep on?
- What do you usually eat for breakfast? Lunch? Dinner?
- Which hand do you use to brush your teeth or your hair?
- Do you always wear your hair in the same style? Which side do you part your hair on?
- What type of clothing do you wear? Do you mostly wear the same colors and styles?
- Who are the people you talk to regularly?
- What kind of music do you listen to?
- How do you get exercise?

In the space below, list your daily routines—especially the ones that have become automatic. The short lines on the right side are for you to use in the next part of this exercise. Just leave them blank for now. If you need additional space, please use the NOTES section at the back of the book.

____ __________

____ __________

____ __________

____ __________

____ __________

____ __________

____ __________

____ __________

____ __________

____ __________

____ __________

____ __________

____ __________

____ __________

____ __________

____ __________

____ __________

Step 2. Once complete, put a check mark on the small line next to the ones you're willing to change up in some way.

That's all you have to do for now. You may want to bookmark this list as you'll be referring to it for the 30-Day Lucky Life Tracker as you put these ideas into action.

Say *Yes* and Go for It!

In Shonda Rhimes' book, *A Year of Saying Yes*, she tells the story of committing to saying *yes* in her life, and how that one choice—and the multitude of others that followed and supported that decision—catapulted her already successful career into an extraordinary one.

Saying *yes* in your life gives you permission to explore new adventures. This requires taking risks—not necessarily daredevil, physical ones like bungee jumping or skydiving, but emotional, professional, or creative risks that stretch you in ways you haven't been willing to stretch before. Going beyond your previous limits dramatically accelerates your personal growth and leads to new opportunities, significantly increasing your chances of being lucky.

Take a Moment to Reflect: In the space below, write your answers to the following questions:

1. What have you said *no* to in your life that now, in hindsight, you wish you'd said *yes* to?

2. Why did you say *no*?
3. If the same situation, or a similar one, happened today, what would you do differently?

____

____

____

____

____

____

Taking Bold Action Means Facing Your Fear

As you probably discovered in the journaling exercise you just did, we usually say *no* to opportunities and invitations because we're afraid—of looking stupid, not being good at something, letting others down, not following through or being flaky, etc. The fear of failure has thwarted many from achieving the life of their dreams.

Yet fear isn't all bad. It serves a purpose: to protect you from harm and keep you alive. Deciding not to jump off a cliff or blithely eat a type of mushroom you're unfamiliar with are certainly wise choices for extending longevity. That's why fear is hardwired into your survival DNA.

The problem is that oftentimes your fears are out of proportion to a situation, or completely unnecessary, because your brain has overreacted to, or even imagined, the threats you face. A big step in overcoming your fears is realizing that most of the things you're afraid of won't really hurt you.

Exercise: Things I've Been Afraid to Try List

Step 1. Take a few minutes and, in the space below, list out all the activities you've wanted to try in your life, but haven't due to fear.

For example: singing, dancing, creating art, playing sports, learning to fly a plane, writing a book, leading a support group, online dating, stand-up comedy, improv classes, etc. Don't overthink it; just write down everything that comes to mind.

If you're stuck or want to explore this from a different angle, ask yourself: *What could I do to add more adventure in my life?* Or complete this sentence: *If I were brave, I would...*

The short lines on the right side are for you to use in the next part of this exercise. Just leave them blank for now. If you need more space, use the NOTES section at the end of the book:

Step 2. Review your list and select the activity you *most want* to try. At this point, don't consider how much that activity scares you; just select the one that speaks to your heart most and put a "1" on the short line to the right of that activity. Continue numbering the activities in the order you most want to try them.

Step 3. Now choose three items from your list that you'd be *willing* to try. This time consider your readiness to face your fears and choose activities that you feel will stretch you but are doable, and write them on the following lines:

____ __________

____ __________

____ __________

____ __________

Step 4. Number the three activities in the order in which you want to do them by writing 1, 2, or 3 on the short line to the right.

After you give these three activities your best shot, select three more. Continue to work your way through all the interests, passions, and adventures you listed.

The next section offers some fear-busters for you to use as you give yourself permission to "feel the fear and to do it anyway."

Getting Past Your Fear

To help you overcome any remaining obstacles to doing the three activities you just selected, we suggest you go through the activities one at a time and apply all three of the following approaches you learned about in *Conscious Luck.*

Approach 1. Respond *rather than* react.

Fear is an unconscious and automatic reaction to a perceived threat. When something frightens us, our survival wiring hijacks us and, within nanoseconds, our bodies go into either fight, flight, or freeze mode, a reaction that can save our lives in the case of real danger.

The problem arises when we stay stuck in the fear even after the danger has passed, and especially when there was never a real danger to begin with. Then this primitive fear mechanism stops us from being and doing all that we aspire to. The solution is to interrupt this reaction, become aware of our fears, and look at them objectively.

Take a Moment to Reflect. Think about the concerns or fears that are stopping you from taking the actions you wrote in Step 3, and then ask yourself: *What's the worst thing that could happen if I did that? Is what I'm afraid will happen* real *or* imagined*? Am I exaggerating the consequences in my head?* Jot down some notes on what you discover here:

____

____

____

____

____

____

When we examine our fears, we discover they're often disproportionate to the situation, and "in the light of day" can be easily managed or dismissed.

Approach 2. Use the breath to switch the body's biochemistry.

As we mentioned in Conscious Luck, fear is often described as "excitement without breath," so the next time you're afraid, just add some breath—and watch your uncomfortable fear transform into pleasurable excitement!

Let's give this formula a test drive: Think of one of the activities you want to do but are too afraid to try. Now close your eyes and visualize yourself doing it. Make it as real as you can. Where are you? Who's with you? What does it feel like?

When the feelings of fear arise, take three long, slow belly-breaths. This will activate your body's parasympathetic response, which will begin to reduce the fear. Remind yourself that you're just imagining the actions that bring up the fear, and that you're safe. Keep breathing slowly and deeply as you continue to rehearse in your mind the successful completion of your goal.

This inner rehearsal of success has been scientifically proven to assist Olympic and other professional athletes in accomplishing their goals. So why not let it work for you? Try it now and, in the space below, note what that experience is like for you.

Approach 3. Face your fear—step by step.

If you investigate your fears, breathe through them, and find you still can't shake your reluctance to take action, what do you do then? If it's something you really want to do—even though it scares you—ask yourself: *Is there a way to do this in smaller steps?*

Say, for example, you've always wanted to sing or perform in front of an audience but are just too afraid. What are some intermediate steps you could take to build comfort around performing for a group? Here are a few ideas:

1. Create a video of you singing and share it with a close friend who loves you and will support you.
2. Sing for an understanding family member.
3. Sing in front of a small group with your eyes closed or facing away from them.
4. Join a chorus or choir and get comfortable singing in front of an audience in the safety of a group.
5. Research voice teachers and schedule a consultation about this problem.

Your turn! Select just one activity from the *Things I've Been Afraid to Try* list you made earlier and commit to taking one small step toward it. It might be writing a first draft of an email to someone you admire and would like to work with, watching a YouTube video on dancing, or reaching out to an encouraging friend and asking them to be your accountability partner as you take on your scary goal.

In the space below, brainstorm some small steps you can take to face your fear:

____

____

____

____

In the next section, we'll actually take one (or more) of those steps.

Summoning Your "Twenty Seconds of Insane Courage"

As you move in the direction of your dreams and goals, you'll encounter occasions that require courage. The good news is that you don't have to be courageous all the time. Just twenty seconds of well-timed bravery—what we call "insane courage"—will do.

Exercise: Priming the Courage Pump

Step 1. ***Remember Past Triumphs.*** Think of moments in your life when you were brave—from the most significant to the most minor. List any situations in which you were insanely courageous for at least 20 seconds or more. It could have been confronting a family member or co-worker about an important matter, learning something new (like riding a bike), overcoming your fear of dogs, asking for a promotion, uncharacteristically speaking up in a meeting, or emailing someone you admire. In the space below, write about at least one such experience, to own the courage you've already displayed in your life.

____

____

____

____

____

____

Step 2. Now, from the list of small steps you wrote in the ***Approach 3. Face your fear—step by step*** section, select one that would take what you consider "insane courage" to attempt and write it here:

___

___

___

___

Step 3. ***Be Your Own Cheerleader.*** Confidence comes in large part from how we talk to ourselves. Imagine being your own best friend or coach. How can you encourage yourself to act on the step you just wrote? What kind, inspiring, loving words can you say to yourself that will initiate action?

Write these words below:

___

___

___

___

Step 4. ***Initiate Liftoff.*** Sometimes being a good coach or friend requires tough love. At those times, you may have to push yourself a bit to cut through your fear and overthinking, and be decisive. To launch yourself into action, author and speaker Mel Robbins suggests counting backwards from 5, NASA-style, and then just going for it. She calls this the 5 Second Rule. It gets you out of your head and into action.

Try it yourself. Right now.

Look at the step you want to take. Do the countdown out loud: 5, 4, 3, 2, 1—and DO IT!

Make the call.
Send the email.
Sing the song.
Sign up for the class.
Record the video and post it.
Ask for help.
Offer support.

Take the action you've been preparing for, and then come back here immediately to do the following journaling.

Take a Moment to Reflect: Bravo! You did it! How did it feel to use your twenty seconds of courage? Close your eyes and savor how it feels to overcome your fears (at least a little). Take a few deep belly-breaths to anchor this experience so you can return it to when necessary.

In the space below, write your experiences and thoughts:

____

____

____

____

____

____

What happened? Write down any result of your action—no matter how small. (You may not have any results yet, which is fine. When you do, capture them here.)

____

____

____

____

____

____

Houston, We Have a Problem

If you still haven't taken action, you may have chosen too big a step, or there's some old conditioning you need to address.

If the step was too big, you'll need to chunk it down further. For example, if your goal is to make a call or send an email, the very first step might be to get the number or the email address. If your goal is to sign up for a class, the very first step might be to research which class is best by doing an internet search and reading reviews and testimonials.

Look at the step you chose and see if you can find an even smaller step inside it. Once you find it, then count backwards from 5 and do that step! Your momentum will usually carry you through to the next step. Keep going!

And if you're still wrestling with blocks from old conditioning, the next exercise will help.

Exercise: Getting to the Root of Your Resistance

Step 1. A good place to start is by identifying the blocks. To facilitate this process, ask yourself the following questions: *What thoughts come up when it's time to act? What's holding me back?* Write your answers below:

____

____

____

____

If you're stuck or want to explore this issue from a different angle, ask yourself these questions:

- Do I need to give myself permission? If so, why?
- Am I waiting for someone else to give me permission? If so, whose permission is it?
- How old is that version of myself that needs permission from someone else? (Generally, blocks that involve needing permission from others stem from childhood.)

Write your answers in the space below:

____

____

____

____

Step 2. Can you give that permission to yourself right now, today? To cement this, fill out the following "permission slip" and then say it aloud:

I, ____________, give myself permission to ______________________________

____

____

Step 3. Now, do the 5 Second Rule countdown and take your one small step!

If you're still stuck, go to Chapter 2 and redo the Upper Limit Problem exercises with your chosen small step in mind. Be patient with yourself. It can take time and repeated effort to unwind your limiting beliefs and mental patterns. The only way you fail is if you quit trying.

What to Do When Your Luck is Stalled

In *Conscious Luck*, you learned about the Luck Vapor Lock, which like the vapor lock in a car's engine, causes you to "stall out" and become stuck in life. At those times, nothing you do seems to be effective, and you don't know how to get back on track. The solution in those situations is to take a break, switch your focus, and help someone else succeed. Giving to others changes your energy, releasing the luck vapor lock and opening up new opportunities for more joy and abundance in your life.

Exercise: Breaking the Luck Vapor Lock

The first step in this process is to stop thinking about yourself and your problems and turn your attention to the people around you.

Step 1. Sit quietly and take three slow, deep belly-breaths. Ask yourself: *Is there anyone I can be of service to or help today?* It can be an old friend, a former client, a relative, a vendor, a neighbor, or anyone else. Note any names or faces that come to mind.

If nothing presents itself, take a few minutes to look through your contacts or your friends on social media. See if you get an energetic hit.

In the space below, write down any names that you discover in this process:

____

____

____

____

____

____

Step 2. Now ask yourself: *How can I help?*

For example:

- Can I buy something from them or support their business in some way?
- Refer a customer or client?
- Write a good review on their website?
- Bring them some food?
- Do an errand or chore for them?
- Offer a listening ear?

What comes up may not make sense to you or may seem silly or too small. Don't judge—just write down any ideas that come to you:

____

____

____

____

____

____

NOTE: If no one or nothing immediately comes to mind, don't worry. Just leave it for now. If you move through your day with these questions in mind, inspired thoughts will appear in their own time. When they do, come back and finish the exercise.

Step 3. Look through your ideas, choose at least one, and take action.

Don't expect instant results—that's not the point. Know you've changed your energy and enjoy the feeling of contributing to others.

Take a Moment to Reflect: How did it feel taking action to help someone else? In the space below, write down your experience:

____

____

____

____

____

____

If you had any breakthroughs or other results after your acts of giving or service, write them here:

____

____

____

Giving from a space of joy breaks the vapor lock on your luck, your love, your happiness, your money supply, your energy, and your creativity. Giving and receiving activate each other. It's a beautiful cycle.

✤

The fifth Conscious Luck Secret tells us that by taking bold action and by finding ways to give to others, you increase your opportunity to experience more good fortune in your life.

In the next chapter on the sixth Conscious Luck Secret, we'll explore how you can improve your luck by being more intentional about the people you spend time with.

6

THE SIXTH SECRET

Find Your Lucky Community

Tell me who your friends are, and I'll tell you who you are.
—Traditional saying

In the beautiful words of John Donne, "No man is an island." All of us spend our lives surrounded by and interacting with many different people. That's why, to increase your luck, it's vital to consider the impact those around you have on you. Your ideas, behaviors, morals, health, and mindset are influenced by the people you associate with, so you want to choose wisely and surround yourself with individuals who uplift you, support you being your best self, and make you luckier.

In *Conscious Luck*, we called this finding your lucky *tribe*. Out of respect for the cultures of native peoples, we have decided to use the term lucky *community* going forward. We think it conveys the same type of inclusiveness and solidarity.

The process of finding your lucky community begins with doing an inventory of everyone you know. The following exercise will help. (If you already did an inventory when reading *Conscious Luck*, please do it again here. You're going to take the exercise a couple of steps further later in this chapter.)

Exercise: Identifying Your Lucky Community

Step 1. Go through all the contacts you have in your address book or smartphone, on your social media pages, on your email server, or on any list of people you spend time with—in person or virtually. As you look at each name, imagine being in that person's presence. Feel what happens in your body. Does that person cause you to tense or relax? Do your eyes light up or do you smile thinking of them? The physiological responses you experience will help in the sorting process.

If you're familiar with Marie Kondo's decluttering book, *The Life-Changing Magic of Tidying Up*, you'll recognize this method. You're sorting the people in your life using essentially the same process Kondo uses to sort belongings: you're looking for that "spark of joy."

Those who inspire that joy have a lucky influence; those who don't, have the opposite effect.

Don't prejudge or assume anything about anyone. Simply use your physical reactions to assist you as you review each name.

Step 2. Once you determine whether a person has a lucky or unlucky influence on you, write their name in the appropriate column below. You'll notice there's a column, which is optional, where you can note how you know that person (for example, from Facebook or LinkedIn, or through your cousin) so you can easily find them in the future.

If there's a chance one of the *Unluckies* will happen upon this book, you can write the names of the people who have an unlucky influence on a separate piece of paper that can be disposed of. Or fill in just the Lucky Influence list.

Lucky Influence:	Unlucky Influence:	How Known:
________________	________________	________________
________________	________________	________________
________________	________________	________________
________________	________________	________________
________________	________________	________________
________________	________________	________________
________________	________________	________________
________________	________________	________________
________________	________________	________________
________________	________________	________________

______________________ ______________________ ______________________

______________________ ______________________ ______________________

Rubber, Meet the Road

Your luck grows when you spend more time, in person or online, with authentically positive, encouraging, and inspiring people, and less time with people who leave you feeling worse after being in their company—either because of their persistent blaming and complaining, or because they are actively unsupportive of your dreams and goals.

Looking at your lists, it should be clear which people you want to spend more time with and which ones you might choose to spend less time with. The problem is that some of the people on the Unlucky Influence List might be difficult or impossible to avoid—they might work with you, be related to you, or even live with you!

It's important to understand that you don't have to cut those people out of your life entirely. We simply recommend spending less time with them if possible, at least until you're strong enough to

1. Recognize and resist the old toxic patterns of trading victim stories and other behaviors that drag down your energy; or
2. Not feel disempowered by their lack of support and approval for your goals and dreams.

If it's not possible to limit your exposure to the people who have an unlucky influence on you, simply being aware of the situation will help. When you're with the Unluckies, we suggest you stop actively participating in any complaining, blaming, or negative gossiping, and also stop sharing your dreams and goals with people who rain on your parade.

IMPORTANT NOTE: It's important to distinguish between an unhealthy relationship based on trading victim stories and blaming others, and a validating relationship in which you listen to each other's stories—which can include feelings of anger, sadness, and fear—and then help each other work through those feelings to become new, empowered versions of yourselves.

There's a big difference between hanging with people who ONLY want to commiserate with you and stay in that negative place, versus surrounding yourself with those who want to support you by hearing your authentic experiences and helping you grow.

As you may have discovered while going through the names of the people in your life, it can also be uncomfortable to spend time with people who are "too positive." As it turns out, it's equally damaging to be around people who strenuously avoid any topic that's not upbeat or happy. Squelching difficult emotions to be more "spiritual" or to escape pain isn't healthy—or helpful.

Your true lucky community understands that you, like everyone, can go through rough patches that bring you down and leave you feeling like a victim. Their role is to support you as you work through your challenges as quickly as you can, and to keep you on track and encourage you to continue taking responsibility for what's going on in your life.

Exercise: Narrowing it Down

Step 1. Using your physical feelings and cues again, go through the people on your Lucky Influence list and place an asterisk (*) by the names of those you *especially* want to spend more time with. Don't second-guess your feelings, and don't worry about whether they'll want to spend more time with you. Just create your wish list.

Step 2. Looking at each of the names with an asterisk, ask yourself: *In what area of my life do I want to engage with this person?* Here are some examples of different possibilities:

- **Social Life**: To meet for walks or meals, to play games or watch movies together, or to read and discuss books.
- **Self-improvement**: To engage as a mentor/mentee or in a mastermind or support group, or as an accountability partner.
- **Fitness or sports**: To serve as a workout buddy or to run, do yoga, or play tennis, golf, basketball, pickleball, or another sport together.
- **Professional Life**: To support career advancement or business success or entrepreneurial aspirations.
- **Hobbies**: To enjoy and discuss common passions and interests, whatever they may be—comic books, backyard chickens, Star Trek, Jane Austen,

politics, Cajun food, etc.

- **Service Projects**: Volunteering together for community clean-ups, food drives, environmental or social justice activism, or other types of do-gooding.

We encourage you to add your own categories if you don't see them here.

Then, place the initials of the area you want to share with each person next to their name. (One person can appear in multiple areas.)

SL – Social Life
SI – Self-Improvement
F/S – Fitness or Sports
PL – Professional Life
H – Hobbies
SP – Service Projects

Step 3. In the space below, brainstorm how you might connect with the members of your Lucky Community more often or deepen your current relationship with them within the categories you chose.

For example: schedule a weekly chess, card, or scrabble game, join the Rotary Club together, have a regular running date, form a gourmet dinner club. The possibilities are endless.

____
____
____
____
____
____
____
____

Optional Step 4. For those Lucky Community members you put in the Self-Improvement category, take a few minutes to feel into whom you'd like

- as an accountability partner—someone you check in with daily or at least a few times a week to report progress toward your goals.
- as a fellow member of a Conscious Luck mastermind group—where you all share wins, lucky stories, and goals on your Conscious Luck journey.
- as a fellow member of a support group, either an established group like Alcoholics Anonymous or Weight Watchers, or a group you form—where you meet to encourage and assist each other to accomplish a specific self-improvement goal like weight loss, sobriety, overcoming grief or abuse, and so on.
- as a mentor—someone who radiates luck and positivity and can support your personal growth one-on-one.

In the space below, write down the names of the people you'd like to approach to share these specific lucky connections:

____

____

____

____

____

____

____

____

A fabulous benefit of including others on your Conscious Luck journey is that you can share your experiences in all areas of life with fellow seekers who can relate to and perhaps advise you, since they're dealing, to a lesser or greater degree, with the same challenges we all face as humans.

Tips for Finding or Expanding your Virtual Lucky Community

One of the blessings of living in an increasingly virtual world is that you can interact with like-minded people in any location around the globe. If you'd like to meet more people to join you on your Conscious Luck journey and you haven't explored the enormous pool of people available through social media, or if you just want to grow your existing virtual community, here are a few ideas:

1. Seek out people who resonate with you on the level of their philosophy, how they communicate about their lives, and what they're up to in the world. To determine this:

   - Look at a person's social media posts.
   - See which groups they belong to.
   - If the person has a website, review it for content and blog posts.

2. Once you find someone who seems like-minded, reach out and initiate communication. Move from email, texts, and other forms of written messages to voice or visual contact (e.g., Zoom, WhatsApp, etc.) as soon as it feels appropriate, so you can experience a deeper, more connected relationship.

3. To facilitate more connection with the people you find:
   - Create a virtual support or mastermind group for one of your chosen life areas that meets regularly to provide help and inspiration to its members.
   - Create a Facebook group that connects, uplifts, and encourages its members.

If you're on Facebook and haven't already joined us, we invite you to be a part of the Conscious Luck Global Community Facebook Group! It's a place to be with your lucky community to:

- Share your Conscious Luck success stories and experiences.
- Interact with authors Gay Hendricks and Carol Kline.
- Hear about Conscious Luck events.
- Ask questions and discuss your wins and challenges.
- Find virtual accountability partners and/or form mastermind groups to support your growing good fortune.

If you are able to access this link, join by clicking on the "Join" button at the top of the page: https://www. consciousluck.com/facebook.

If you're reading this in a hard-copy book, go to Facebook, search for "Conscious Luck Global Community," and press the "Join" button there.

Accelerating Your Conscious Luck Journey through Personal Development

Expanding your personal growth activities and your support network will definitely fast-track your good fortune. Personal development helps you overcome negative conditioning and limiting beliefs with the guidance of wise, insightful, and lucky people—either through their books, seminars, audio programs or videos, or by signing up for their online classes. Reading the autobiographies, biographies, or memoirs of real-life heroes—past or present—is also an enriching and inspiring activity. Dedicating just 15–30 minutes a day to soaking up wisdom and connecting with greatness can have a profound effect on the trajectory of your life.

Take a Moment to Reflect: On the following lines, list any personal development leaders you'd like to learn from, teachers and thinkers who intrigue or attract you, books or programs you are interested in or that have been recommended to you, or anything else that could advance your knowledge, confidence, and skills:

____

____

____

____

____

____

Keep adding to this list as you discover more personal development resources you want to explore. It's helpful to have one place to keep track of them all.

If money is an issue, visit your local or virtual online library to check out books. There are also a great number of free or low-cost personal development resources online that can help you get started. Visit authors' and transformational leaders' websites, subscribe to their newsletters and YouTube channels, and follow them on Facebook and Instagram to learn more.

In the following section, you're going to do another type of inventory—one that will help you see your luck profile in a more holistic context.

Whole-Life Luckiness

A wonderful adjunct to the Luck-Worthy Goals processes you did in Chapter 4 is to complete the following Wheel of Life Luck Inventory. This inventory allows you to evaluate your current level of luck in each of the areas of your life. It's also a wonderful tool for sharing your goals and enlisting specific support from your lucky community.

Exercise: The Wheel of Life Luck Inventory

Using a scale of 1 – 10 (1 being the lowest and 10 the highest), take a moment to score yourself on how lucky you feel in each of the following areas. In the space provided, make a few quick notes about how you arrived at that score.

Spiritual Life/Contribution to Others: ____________________

____

____

____

Family/Relationships: ____________________

____

____

____

Mental Development/Education: ____________________

____

____

____

Emotional Balance/Self-Care: ________________

____

____

____

Health and Wellness/Physical Fitness: ________________

____

____

____

Career/Professional Growth: ________________

____

____

____

Financial/Wealth Creation: ________________

____

____

____

Home/Physical Surroundings: ________________

____

____

____

Fun/Social Life/Recreation and Adventure: ________________

____

____

____

Now that you've assessed where you are, you can begin creating a Whole-Life Luck Acceleration Plan to catapult you into the realm of *whole-life luckiness.*

Your Whole-Life Luck Acceleration Plan

The first step of any plan is to get clear on the outcome you want to create. In this case, that means clarifying what you want in all aspects of your life—*especially* in the areas in which you gave yourself low scores.

Step 1: For each of the areas below, ask yourself: *What does being lucky in this area mean to me?* For those areas that need improvement, ask: *What would I like to experience more of in that area?*

In the space below, write down what a score of 8 or above in each area would look like for you:

Spiritual Life/Contribution to Others:

____

____

____

Family/Relationships:

____

____

____

Mental Development/Education:

____

____

____

Emotional Balance/Self-Care:

____

____

____

Health and Wellness/Physical Fitness:

Career/Professional Growth:

Financial/ Wealth Creation:

Home/Physical Surroundings:

Fun/Social Life/Recreation and Adventure:

Congratulations! You're now in a great position to make progress, having both points on the map that you need in order to chart a route: 1) You know where you are, and 2) You know where you want to go. In Step 2, you'll brainstorm specific goals and action steps that will take you to your lucky destination.

Step 2: Review your answers in Step 1, focusing most on the areas in which you scored lower than 5. Ask yourself, *What can I do to get where I want to go?*

Start by identifying specific goals. For example, if I scored below 5 in the area of Health and Wellness/Physical Fitness and I pinpointed "being at my ideal weight of ___ and being in shape" as being lucky in that area, the specific goals I could set might be 1) lose five pounds over the next two months and 2) start working out regularly.

Write your goals below:

____

____

____

____

____

____

Step 3. Come up with as many action steps as you can for the goals you just set. If you set a lot of goals, select one that you want to work on first and focus on creating action steps for it. You can come back to this section to select new goals and create corresponding action steps as you complete the previous ones.

In our example of losing 5 pounds, one action step could be going through your refrigerator, freezer, and cupboards to get rid of unhealthy and fattening foods. Throw them away or, if that feels too wasteful, give them away. Another might be to go shopping for healthy foods, like whole grains and fresh fruits and vegetables, to restock your larder.

Write your action steps below:

____

____

____

____

____

____

If these goals (and action steps) are different than the ones you selected to work on in Chapter 4, evaluate how important these ones are in relation to the Chapter 4 goals.

If they are more or equally important, slot these action steps into your 30-day Tracker instead of or along with the action steps you identified for your 30-day goal.

If these goals are less important to you right now, review this section again when you complete your 30-day goal, and re-evaluate these goals again then.

If you need more clarity on your priorities, use the Conscious Luck Heart Meditation in Chapter 4 to check in with your deeper self.

Keep these goals and action steps in mind as you interact with, and enlist the support of, your lucky community, including your accountability partner, your mastermind group, or your mentor.

We suggest you redo the Wheel of Life Luck Inventory and Luck Acceleration Plan at significant times of the year, such as on your birthday, or at the beginning of a new year. This gives you an opportunity to acknowledge your growth and to set the intention for what you'd like to create more of in the future.

♣

In the next chapter, we'll explore how to be your most aligned, authentic self, and learn how that increases your *luck quotient*.

7

THE SEVENTH SECRET

Learn to Be at the Right Place at the Right Time

Most of us would agree that "being at the right place at the right time" is a big part of being lucky. In *Conscious Luck*, you learned the formula for arriving at those fortunate coordinates more consistently: *Listen to your internal GPS.*

In the following pages, we'll take a deeper dive into the three foundational components of that GPS—finding your essence pace, developing your intuition, and clarifying your values.

As discussed in previous chapters, an important key to increasing your luck is to own how and when you've already been lucky in your life. In this chapter, you're going to do that again, this time focusing specifically on your right-place/right-time experiences.

Exercise: Owning Your Right-Place/Right-Time Luck

Take a few minutes to think back over your life and recall as many examples as you can of being at the right place at the right time.

Here are a few real-life stories people have shared:

- I happened to be in the lobby of an office building while I was traveling in another state, and I ran into one of my idols—this unexpected encounter later resulted in us working together.
- My husband and I were in the market for new e-bikes, so my husband had been doing quite a bit of research on them. One day, on a beach walk,

we veered off our normal path and spoke with a guy who had a brand of e-bike my husband had never heard of. The guy raved about it, and when we got home and looked at reviews, we found they averaged 4.8 out of 5! If we'd gone to a bike shop as we'd planned, we may never have heard about this bike, because it's sold only online.

- Walking home from the local grocery store, I took a different route than usual, and crossed paths with a stranger who ended up becoming a close friend and an important part of my professional network.

On the following lines, list as many of your own stories as possible. Write a sentence or two, or just label them with a summary title. You don't have to write the whole story out.

____

____

____

____

____

____

____

____

Now that you've documented some of your past right-place/right-time events, let's amp up your ability to create them more consciously in the future. We'll start by reviewing the component of your internal GPS that we call your "essence pace"—the ability to move your body through space at a rate that's in harmony with your center and connected to the present moment.

Your Essence Pace

On page 126 of *Conscious Luck*, we focused on the "moving through space" aspect of your essence pace:

> Operating at the speed of luck requires finding the stride that allows you to be present in *both* mind and body right where you are—in the moment

happening *now*. You're not out in front of the moment or being dragged behind it.

We call that stride your "essence pace"—the speed at which you can move through space with a happy, sincere smile on your face. You can be moving quickly or slowly, but always with a sense of grounded ease. The key element is that you aren't stressed or anxious. When you move at your essence pace, you'll certainly enjoy yourself more and, in our experience, you're also more likely to arrive at the optimal spot at just the right time.

Moving at your essence pace requires awareness—and practice. If you're like most people, you read about the essence pace in *Conscious Luck*, and thought, *Wow, that's interesting*, and then kept reading. Maybe you've thought about it since then, but chances are you haven't incorporated it into your daily life.

To make moving at your essence pace a habit—like working out or eating well—you've got to commit to practicing it, establish what it feels like in your body, and then remind yourself to do it every day until it becomes more ingrained and habitual. To facilitate this process, we recommend you do the following exercise.

Exercise: Establishing Your Essence Pace

Step 1. **Committing to Moving at Your Essence Pace.** You know the whys of committing, and the hows—desire, willingness, and then commitment—so let's just get to it.

On the lines below, write out the following three sentences, putting your name in the blank space:

I, ________________, want to move at my essence pace.
I, ________________, am willing to move at my essence pace.
I, ________________, commit to practice moving at my essence pace.

____

____

____

Now that you've declared your intention to move at the speed of luck, the next step is to establish a baseline experience to build on. (If you've done the following exercise before, that's fine. Please do it again. Your baseline can change over time.)

*Step 2: **Finding Your Essence Pace.*** Let's take a walk. If you can't do it right now, please take a break and come back to this as soon as you're ready. It's great to walk outside, but if that's not possible, it's fine to walk inside your home or office. Experiment with speeding up and slowing down and varying the movement from minute to minute. You might be going uphill or downhill, climbing or descending stairs, but always follow your inner guidance to go either more quickly or more slowly. It may take several attempts to find your essence pace while you're moving at different speeds, so keep experimenting.

A key element of your essence pace is that you're able to breathe easily and smile sincerely. When you find that pace, take time to feel what it's like to be right here, right now, at ease in your own body, and aware of what's around you as you walk. Once you're clear how your essence pace feels, take a moment to "mark it" in your mind and body.

Take a Moment to Reflect: Were you able to clearly experience moving at your essence pace? If so, how did it feel in your body? Did any specific emotions or sensations come up for you? For example, maybe you experienced a calm alertness, joy, increased energy or heightened sensory perception, peace, or something else entirely. Did you feel any resistance? Did moving at your essence pace feel cumbersome or slow you down when you wanted to hurry?

Write your answers in the space below:

____

____

____

____

____

____

____

If you're used to multi-tasking as you walk—"chewing on" the past or planning the future—being mentally present *where you are* can take some getting used to. But the benefits of integrating your mind and body as you move, including taking in additional sensory information from your environment and arriving at your destination relaxed and centered, will more than make up for a few minutes of lost speed or analysis.

A New Twist to Your Essence Pace—A Stationary Version

Just as there's an essence pace for moving your body from one place to another, there's also an essence pace for sitting or standing still, which we call your stationary essence pace. Your stationary essence pace requires the same coordination of mind and body, and the same anchoring to your core, whether you're sitting (or standing) at a desk, staring for hours at a screen while absorbed in cyberspace, or standing behind a counter or in front of a classroom or conference room.

The most important attribute of an essence pace—moving or stationary—is your ability to let go of any agitations, worries, stresses, or distractions, and re-establish more balance, peace, and connection between your inner and outer worlds.

So, while sitting or standing, if you find yourself overwhelmed, anxious, jittery, unable to focus, or simply not present to the physical reality around you, that's the time to find your stationary essence pace. This stationary centering process is just as effective for being in the right place at the right time as the one you do while moving, so use it as another way to increase your luck.

Exercise: Finding Your Stationary Essence Pace

The following exercise will help you connect to your stationary essence pace when stressors, anxiety, or spaciness arise. Read through the steps once and then do the exercise.

When you become aware of any agitation or disconnection:

1. Stop what you're doing.
2. If you're sitting, place both feet flat on the ground. If you're standing, place your feet shoulder-width apart.

3. Close your eyes and take three or more deep belly-breaths to calm and ground yourself.
4. If you're sitting, rest your hands, palms up, on top of your thighs. If standing, simply let your hands hang easily by your sides.
5. As you slowly breathe in through your nose, open your hands fully, timing the movement to end with the conclusion of the "in" breath. Your fingers should be straight and spread as wide as possible as you finish inhaling. Think "jazz hands."
6. Then, as you slowly exhale through the nose, gradually relax your hands, letting your fingers curl into a loose fist. Coordinate finishing your exhale with finishing the hand movement.
7. Repeat the process 3 or 4 times, or until you feel more relaxed and more fully present in your body, mind, and the moment happening "right now."

Take a Moment to Reflect: Did you notice a shift in your mood as you consciously coordinated your breath and movement? Did you feel calmer, more centered in yourself, or more grounded in this moment? In the space below, please jot down what you experienced.

____

____

____

____

____

____

Like your moving essence pace, your stationary one simultaneously creates more relaxation and more alertness. It allows your mind to stop ping-ponging between the past and the future so that you can pay attention to what's taking place in the present—both within you and in your environment.

This is a great exercise to do when you notice you're feeling disturbed or spacey, but you can also do it proactively, whenever you want to be more centered and focused: between meetings, before a zoom call, after a long day of work, or anytime you're transitioning from one activity to the next.

Find a downloadable PDF of this exercise at www.consciousluck.com/workbook that you can print and put in your wallet or on your computer to keep the steps handy for use whenever you need them.

Practicing Your Pace

To establish your essence pace as a part of your daily routine, it's important to practice finding it regularly. In the space below, brainstorm ways you can remind yourself to consistently connect to your essence pace, while moving or while stationary, until it becomes more natural and habitual. Here are some ideas:

- Set an alarm on your phone to pop-up at least two or three times a day with the message: "Are you operating at your essence pace?" This will remind you to check in with yourself.
- If you have a smartwatch or a wearable fitness tracking device with apps that alert you to take deep breaths or stand up and stretch throughout the day, use those same reminders to remind you to connect to your essence pace.
- Place Post-it notes that say "Find Your Essence Pace" on your bathroom mirror, the door of your closet, the refrigerator, your car dashboard, your computer monitor, your coffee mug, or your water glass or bottle.
- Have a T-shirt made that says, "I'm Moving at the Speed of Luck," and wear it when you go for a walk or run.
- Alert your accountability partner that you will text them each night to report how many times you checked in with yourself about your essence pace that day.
- Add the affirmation, "I'm always operating at the speed of luck," to your morning and evening Conscious Luck meditations.

Write your ideas here:

____

____

____

____

____

____

The rewards of consciously cultivating your essence pace are enormous: it brings you into the present moment, centers you in your body, and opens you to the inner guidance that you need to be luckier.

Now let's take a deeper look at where that inner guidance comes from.

Following Your Intuition

The next setting on your internal GPS is your intuition—that still, small voice inside that knows what to do and where to go to be at the right place at the right time. Some people refer to intuition as instinct or gut sense.

We all have intuition, but not everyone hears it or trusts it enough to utilize it. The exercises that follow will help you:

- Increase your perception of your intuition
- Build your faith in its wisdom and reliability
- Learn to put it to use in your daily life

Even if your intuition is already strong and well developed, these exercises may provide new understanding and techniques, so we encourage you to give them a try.

Take a Moment to Reflect: What's your relationship with your intuition? Think of times when you acted on a "feeling" about someone, an impulse to go somewhere, or a hunch to do something—and magic happened as a result. For example:

- You called the person you had a feeling about, and they said, "I was just about to call you," facilitating a valuable conversation.
- You followed your impulse or hunch and it put you in the perfect spot to run into someone you needed to see or have always wanted to meet.

- You listened to your intuition and it saved you from inconvenience. Perhaps you acted on a feeling to grab your keys when you went outside to empty the trash and, sure enough, when you returned, the door you'd propped open had accidently shut and locked itself.

Write your experiences here:

____

____

____

____

____

____

Next, recall any times you had hunches, feelings, and impulses you *didn't* heed, and then suffered the consequences of ignoring your intuition. For example:

- You had an uneasy feeling about someone but ignored it and got hurt.
- You *just knew* the stock your broker recommended was a bad investment, but you bought it anyway, only to watch it plummet.
- You had an impulse to take a different route on your morning commute but second-guessed yourself—and got stuck in a massive traffic jam because of an accident on the road you took.

Write your experiences here:

____

____

____

____

____

____

If your intuition isn't something you value, simply explore your feelings about that. Do you even believe in intuition? Are you afraid of it? Has following a hunch or a feeling about something ever led you astray?

In the space below, write down any experiences, insights, or ideas about your intuition that surface:

____

____

____

____

____

____

____

____

No matter what your experience has been up until now, it's 100 percent possible to develop and deepen your intuition or gut sense and enjoy the benefits of this highly effective means of perception. All it takes is intention, attention, and practice.

Discovering Your Sixth Sense

Most of us have been trained to think logically and analytically—to take one mental step after another in a linear progression. Remember having to "show your work" when you solved a math problem in school? The emphasis on linear learning often stops us from recognizing and accepting knowledge that comes to us in flashes, fragments, and bursts. Though not strictly logical, the information we receive this way "feels" right at a deeper level. When we understand that intuition is not supernatural or mystical, but simply a different way of processing data, it removes the "woo-woo" factor.

To start the process of discovering your sixth sense, simply have the intention to be open to any intuitive messages you receive. Because intuition comes from a source beyond your conscious, rational mind, perceiving it requires a different kind of attention.

The simplest way to hear that still, small voice is to get quiet and listen for it. There are many ways to do this. Here are a few ideas:

Journaling

Using a pen and paper, do some "automatic writing." Ask yourself a question such as, *What do I need to know now*? or *What should I do?* about a specific decision you have to make, and then write whatever comes up. Don't judge or overthink it. It doesn't have to make sense. You don't have to act on what you write. Just keep your hand moving for at least five minutes. You can use a computer but writing by hand stimulates more areas of the brain than using a keyboard and is more powerful for creative thinking.

When you feel finished, take a break and then review what you wrote. See if anything surprising or useful emerged. Don't be discouraged if little of value appeared. It may take some time to experience the benefits of this practice. Whatever you wrote, the exercise is useful for deepening your ability to listen to your inner voice innocently and without judgment.

Sit Quietly/Meditate

Reducing your mental static is crucial for noticing the hunches, insights, and feelings—emotional and physical—that are the building blocks of intuition.

To practice accessing your intuition, set aside 10 or 15 minutes of "me" time, and sit in a place where you won't be disturbed. Then, close your eyes and do some belly-breathing for a few minutes.

As your mind and body relax, become aware of the thoughts passing through your mind. Imagine that you're sitting on the bank of a river and your thoughts are like leaves floating by on the surface of the water. Don't get involved with any of the thoughts—just observe them as they come…and then go.

In this quiet state, mentally ask yourself an open question like the ones suggested in the journaling approach above. For example, *What do I need to know now? What should I do? What's my next step?* Select a question and, once you ask it, simply notice *the very first thought* that arises. Don't judge, question, or dismiss the thought. Just register the thought and keep sitting quietly. Follow the thought wherever it leads, noting any feelings that appear.

When you feel complete, take a few more belly-breaths and then slowly open your eyes. Have a pen and pad of paper ready to write down the messages you received. Repeat the process for each question you want to pose.

We recommend learning a formal meditation technique and practicing it daily. This will establish a more continuous state of inner calm and stillness and make it easier for you to notice intuitive hunches on an ongoing basis. (For links to specific meditation programs we recommend, go to the Resources section.)

Take a Hot Shower or Bath

The feel and sound of water relax your body—and quiet your mind. In the shower, close your eyes and let the water wash over you. As it flows down your body and into the drain, let any anxiety, tension, and mental chatter flow away along with the water.

In the bath, add essential oils to the water to soothe your senses and, if you like, put on soothing instrumental music to disengage your analytical mind. Close your eyes and take a few deep, slow belly-breaths.

Then, whether showering or bathing, ask yourself any open questions you'd like and, again, listen for your first response. Afterward, write down anything that came up.

Do Something Mindless

Have you ever heard the saying, "Busy hands, empty mind, full heart"? In monasteries, convents, and ashrams around the globe, doing daily physical tasks like gardening, cleaning, cooking, and chopping wood is a time-honored tradition. The chores provide welcome physical exercise after the long hours the monks and nuns spend in meditation and prayer, but they also help balance the mind, body, and emotions, leaving the practitioners receptive to the deepest and most delicate impulses of their inner life.

To create the same powerful dynamic for yourself, choose activities that involve paying some attention, but for the most part, leave your mind free to roam. Here are some examples:

- Chop vegetables
- Knit or crochet

- Wash dishes
- Iron
- Rake leaves
- Pull weeds in the garden
- Go for a run
- Be creative: paint, draw, dance, sculpt, or sing.

You get the idea. Engage in any pursuits that get you out of your head and stimulate more whole-body, heart-based, or right-brain activity. As your mind settles down, introduce an open question of your choice and be attentive to your first impulse.

Whichever methods you choose, don't be discouraged if you don't have much success at first. Keep going. The more you practice listening to your intuition, the better you'll get at hearing it.

Take a Moment to Reflect: Review the ideas for accessing your intuition offered above and then, in the space below, select the ones that appeal to you the most and write them down. Feel free to add any others that come to your mind.

____

____

____

____

____

____

From now on, make a point of including these activities as often as possible to your daily routine.

Acting on Intuitive Guidance

Being quiet enough inside to receive flashes of intuition is only part of the equation. It's equally important to *act* on those insights and then evaluate the results of those actions. Connecting your inner guidance to subsequent positive outcomes will increase your confidence in your own intuitive skills.

Here are some suggestions to help you practice *acting* on your intuition in different situations. We recommend using the NOTES section in the back of the workbook to jot down what happens as a result:

1. **Driving.** If you're driving to a destination and there are multiple routes to get there, before you start the car, ask yourself, *Which way should I go?* Listen for any impulses, hunches, or mental pictures, and then take action. Note anything that happens as a result.

   Did your choice lead to any luck? For example:

   - You arrived in record time.
   - You avoided a traffic jam caused by emergency road repair on your normal route.
   - You spotted a store that carries your favorite brand of clothing or camping equipment that you'd didn't know was there
   - You found a new park or golf course you'd like to visit.

Many people find that using their intuition in this way allows them to discover new treasures and adventures in their local area, even if they've lived there for many years and know it well.

2. **Dressing.** Before you get dressed for work or an event, take a deep breath to center yourself. Looking into your closet or just thinking about your clothes, ask yourself, *What should I wear today?* Pay attention to your first thought.

You might have an impulse to wear something dressier than normal, or less dressy, or you might be attracted to a certain color. Don't second-guess yourself. Take action based on your first thought and pay attention to what occurs. For example:

- If you were led to wear something dressier than usual, did you happen to run into the president of your company or another important person in your life? Did you see someone you wanted to make a good impression on? Were you called into an unexpected meeting and felt more comfortable than you would have if you'd worn your usual attire?

- If you were guided to dress less formally than usual, did you find that this decision turned out to be appropriate due to some unanticipated situation you found yourself in? Did your more casual clothing come in handy in some way—perhaps because you were asked to help move something or you had to clean up a spill?
- Did someone comment on the color that you were led to wear? Did it make a difference to your day in any way?

3. **Checking Your Mail or the News.** When going through your email inbox, scrolling through articles on your news feed, sorting your snail mail, or reading a magazine or newspaper, pay attention to any instantaneous responses or gut feelings you have to any aspect of an email, letter, or article, and act accordingly. Note any results that follow your action. For example:

- Although you get a lot of junk email, for some reason you're drawn to a particular email or letter from an unfamiliar source. Rather than discard it as you normally might, when you open it, you find it contains information that's useful for a special project you're working on.
- A news story that catches your eye leads you to an important connection or event that helps you personally or professionally.

The key is paying attention at the instant the intuition arises, registering it before it passes and is dismissed and forgotten. Building this faculty of immediate attention will help you heed the cues of your intuition.

Following through on your hunches and inspirations with action is essential for increasing your ability to be at the right place at the right time, so make a commitment to practice this process in the coming days and weeks.

To do this, take a few moments each day to center yourself by taking three deep belly-breaths, then using one of the suggestions offered in this section, or an original idea of your own, practice connecting to and acting on your intuition, and take note of what occurs. After doing this for at least a week or two, come back to this page and do the following journaling.

Take a Moment to Reflect. Did following your intuition lead you to more luck? Did you find that it became easier and more natural the more you practiced? Did you find any resistance to trying this? In the space below, write down anything you learned or experienced by following the suggestions or your own ideas:

____

____

____

____

____

____

____

____

If you find yourself *not* taking an action you were guided to take and realize later that you would have benefited from that action, don't beat yourself up. Just recognize it, use it as motivation to trust yourself more in the future, and make a commitment to take the next intuition-inspired action.

Too often, our craving to be right and our fear of being wrong limit our life and our luck. Give yourself permission to take chances, make mistakes, test things out, and grow from your experiences.

Be True to Yourself

The final setting on your internal GPS is your integrity or "moral compass." When you take action guided by your integrity, *who you are inside* matches *what you do outside.*

In *Conscious Luck*, Cydney Davis's story of how she became a back-up singer for Marvin Gaye exemplified how being at the right place at the right time happens far more often when you act as the person you most want to be—in alignment with your values, passions, and priorities. Greater flow, synchronicities, and ultimately more luck appear when your deepest principles guide your decisions and your life.

The first step to living by your values is identifying them clearly. Most of us have a general idea of our values and priorities, but they can change over time, and it's important to revisit them periodically. To make sure your understanding of your own values is current and specific, we suggest you do the following exercise.

Exercise: What are Your Values, and How Do You Express Them?

Step 1. Take some time now to identify the values, standards, and nonnegotiable principles you embrace—for example: honesty, fairness, generosity, taking responsibility, courtesy, and kindness—and their expressions, or how they play out in your behavior.

To assist you, here's a list of examples of both values and their expressions. Circle those that resonate with you and, in the blank spaces provided at the end of the list, add any others that are important to you but not listed here.

- Being friendly to strangers
- Making people feel included and welcome
- Being kind to animals
- Being kind to people
- Being honest
- Practicing the Golden Rule
- Giving others the benefit of the doubt
- Being responsible
- Leaving anywhere I go better than how I found it (cleaner, more beautiful, more organized)
- Being a lifelong learner
- Being grateful
- Appreciating others
- Honoring people's space and opinions
- Being courteous to and considerate of others
- Being vegetarian or vegan
- Not investing in, buying from, or supporting companies that violate my values

- Standing up for myself
- Expressing my creative talents
- Protecting the environment/living sustainably
- Eating nutritious, organic, locally sourced food
- Following the rules designed to protect society
- Upholding justice
- Being courageous
- Helping others and being of service
- Communicating clearly and effectively
- Choosing long-term satisfaction over immediate gratification
- Thinking outside the box—committing to thinking creatively, being as adaptable as possible, or keeping an open mind
- Being a good parent
- ______________________________
- ______________________________
- ______________________________
- ______________________________
- ______________________________
- ______________________________
- ______________________________
- ______________________________

Step 2. Explore this question from a different angle by examining your responses to actual behaviors—yours and others'. (This step is based on a values-clarifying exercise from life coach, speaker, and author Ritu Bhasin: https://ritubhasin.com/blog/values-based-living.)

Take some time to reflect on recent events in your life—personal or professional—and on other people's actions that have made an impression on you, whether you know the people personally or heard about them in the media. In the spaces below, record *at least one* event in each of the following categories. There may be some overlap, and it's okay to list the same event in different categories.

Things you did that made you feel good (For example, you helped your neighbor, cleaned out your garage, or earned a promotion at work.)

____

____

____

Things you did that made you feel bad (For example, you binged on chocolate, had a fight with a friend, or yelled at your child.)

____

____

____

Things you did that made you feel useful (For example, you helped your neighbor, called your senator about an upcoming bill, or showed up for a friend in pain.)

____

____

____

Things that *others* did that you admired (For example, someone stood up for what they believed in, a friend published a book after years of work, a celebrity donated a large sum of money to help disaster victims.)

____

____

____

Things that *others* did that you disapproved of or that made you angry (For example, a public figure was caught in an ethics scandal, your daughter was bullied at school, a work associate took credit for your idea.)

____

Look at your answers and ask yourself the following questions, looking for any underlying patterns or themes.

1. *Were there any similarities among the positive events you listed?* For example, were the things that you felt good about doing, that made you feel useful, or that you admired about others' actions related to kindness, generosity, courage, or creativity?

2. *How about the challenging things?* What values or standards were violated by yours or others' actions? If injustice or rudeness or lack of discipline irked you, then the opposite—justice, kindness, or inner strength—is a value or standard you hold dear.

Based on your answers thus far, as well as the list from Step 1, use the following space to write down what you've discovered about your values, standards and nonnegotiable principles.

Finally, in the space below, as simply and clearly as possible, write down what you feel are your most important core values:

Over the next few days and weeks, check in with yourself frequently as you make decisions—small and large—and use your newfound clarity about what's important to you to ask: *Is this action in line with my values?* Your intention to keep your values on your radar makes it far more likely that you'll act in harmony with them.

And while we firmly believe that living a values-based life will make you luckier, we can *guarantee* you'll feel more empowered and at peace when "your insides" match "your outsides"!

✤

As you've seen, the seventh Conscious Luck Secret is about 1) feeling centered while moving and stationary, 2) noticing and heeding intuitive cues, and 3) living in alignment with your personal integrity. Mastering these techniques will enhance your ability to intentionally increase your good fortune.

In the next and last secret, you'll explore how to practice gratitude and appreciation in ways that significantly expand your lucky opportunities.

8

THE EIGHTH SECRET

Practice Radical Gratitude and Appreciation

If you had to choose just one Conscious Luck Secret to master, the eighth Secret is the one. As you learned in *Conscious Luck*, the ability to be truly grateful and appreciative draws more luck to you—on a practical, as well as an energetic, level.

When you feel grateful for the gifts you receive, and express appreciation for your good fortune and the beauty around you, everyone—even the universe itself—wants to give you more. We're sure you've experienced this too: If you go out of your way to help someone or give them a gift and they thank you and tell you how appreciative they are, don't you want to give even more to that person? But if they don't say thank you or express appreciation, how likely are you to want to give to them again? Being grateful attracts more to be grateful for!

Another benefit of practicing gratitude and appreciation on a regular basis is that it enables you to find the luck in every situation—even when it's buried in your most difficult challenges. Combine that with the ability to attract more luck, and you can see why cultivating greater gratitude and appreciation ensures more good fortune in your life.

In *Conscious Luck*, we made an important distinction between gratitude and appreciation:

> **Gratitude is something you feel.** Gratitude is *feeling* thankful for the people, places, and events that enrich your life, including your health, your relationships, your possessions, and your talents and gifts.
>
> **Appreciation is something you do.** Appreciation is an active process, done either internally, using attention, or externally, through expression. Appreciation can be practiced at any time.

Appreciation can also be the gateway to gratitude. If you have difficulty feeling grateful, start with appreciation. The next exercise will show you how.

Internal Appreciation: Awareness and Attention are Essential

When we appreciate something internally, we focus on it deeply to perceive its qualities, whether it's art, music, our spouse or friend, a scene in nature, or a good meal. On a physiological level, appreciation opens the body, making the breath fuller and perception richer—all our senses are heightened because we're giving them more attention.

In the book, we suggested an appreciation activity to try. We repeat it here in a more structured form. The following exercise is a great way to get in touch with the basics of appreciation and will serve as the foundation of further work in the chapter.

Exercise: Focusing Your Attention

Right now, wherever you are, look around and choose an object, scene, or individual to focus on. Examine whatever you chose carefully, noting all the positive qualities you observe.

If you've chosen a tangible object, appreciate the vibrancy of its colors, the beauty of its design, and the artistry of its creator.

If you're outdoors and focusing on natural beauty, savor the quality of the light, the scent of flowers, or the breeze touching your skin.

Or perhaps you've chosen the sweet, familiar face of your pet at your feet, your child's joy as he or she plays with toys, or the animated gestures of a beloved friend or family member.

Feel the value of whatever it is you're focusing on in this moment.

In the space below, capture as best you can all that you appreciate about the object of your attention:

____

____

____

____

____

Take A Moment to Reflect: How do you feel in your body, mind, and emotions after doing this appreciation exercise?

Next, we're going to practice appreciating someone very important in your life: *you*!

Exercise: Turning the Stream of Appreciation on Yourself

Have you ever watched a young child look at their reflection in a mirror? Children smile, gaze directly into their own eyes, dance around, and sometimes even kiss their own reflected face. They appreciate themselves with such openness and ease. Now, think of how you view your reflection. Can you appreciate yourself with the same openness and ease? To find out, you're going to do another version of the previous exercise, this time focusing on yourself as the object of appreciation.

Take a few minutes now to appreciate and celebrate YOU. Imagine you are your own best friend and, in the space below, inventory your good qualities and strengths—physical, mental, emotional, and spiritual. This can include your contributions to others, your talents and skills, all your accomplishments in life, and anything else you can think of. Look deeply for all the ways you are a gift and blessing in the world.

____

____

____

Take A Moment to Reflect: How did that feel? Was it easy or difficult? In the space below, jot down your internal reaction to appreciating yourself:

____

____

____

____

____

____

If appreciating yourself was easy and enjoyable, that's great! This indicates a healthy amount of self-love, which, as you know from chapter 2, helps you feel more worthy of luck.

If appreciating yourself was hard for you, make this exercise a regular part of your day (or week) until you feel comfortable looking at yourself with the same appreciative eye you're cultivating toward others.

External Appreciation: Expression is the Key

Now that you've discovered qualities to appreciate in others, the next step is to express that appreciation. Expressing appreciation comes with a host of benefits: it develops deeper relationships, fosters collaboration, and helps you stand out from the crowd. People remember people who appreciate them and are more likely to be helpful and supportive in return.

Communicating your appreciation on a regular basis also increases your open-heartedness, a quality that makes you a more attractive person energetically. All these benefits contribute directly to you experiencing better luck.

Even knowing all that, we often don't get around to writing a thank-you note (or even just an email), or to calling someone to tell them how much we appreciate their gift, their support, or their friendship. Due mainly to our busy lives, our good intentions simply don't translate into action.

Because of this widespread tendency to put off expressing appreciation, we recommend that you make it a priority to do all the steps of the following exercise, especially Step 3, which is *immediately following through.* Being a great appreciator is a proven way to be luckier, so why not put it to work for you? This next exercise is designed to help you hone your appreciation skills.

Exercise: Enhancing Your Appreciation Skills

Step 1: ***Who Are the People you Want to Thank?***

List below the names of everyone you would like to thank or have been meaning to thank. These could be friends, your spouse, a child, an employee or an employer, your favorite server at a restaurant, the owner of the local bakery, or anyone at all whom you would like to acknowledge for their contribution to you, your family, your community, or the world. If you need more space to write, we suggest you go to the NOTES section at the back of the book so you can keep all the names together in one place.

______________________________	______________________________
______________________________	______________________________
______________________________	______________________________
______________________________	______________________________
______________________________	______________________________
______________________________	______________________________
______________________________	______________________________
______________________________	______________________________
______________________________	______________________________
______________________________	______________________________
______________________________	______________________________

Looking at this list, choose one person from your list to thank right now, either verbally or in writing.

Write their name here ________________________________

Step 2: ***Make Your Thank You the Best it Can Be***

The hallmark of a great *thank you* is that the thanker deepens their appreciation for what they have received, and the thankee feels acknowledged and fully seen.

Our friend, author and relationship expert Alison Armstrong, says there are three gifts within every gift, whether it's a physical object, an act of service, or an experience: 1) the gift itself, 2) the motivation of the giver, and 3) the impact of the gift. Take some time to identify these three aspects before you thank your selected person, by reflecting on the following questions:

1. **The Gift Itself**: What was the gift exactly?

   If it was a physical object, note as many of its features as possible—the color, the shape, the material, the quality.

   If the gift was an act of service, what did that person do for you specifically? What efforts did they make?

   If the gift was an experience, like sharing a meal or being taken to a show or museum, take note of the environment, the flavors, or the companionship and conversation.

2. **The Motivation of the Giver**: What compelled the giver to give you the gift? Honor the motivation—the thoughts and feelings—behind the gift. For example: appreciate the giver for caring enough to give to you, for wanting to help you, or for the concern they felt that prompted them to use their resources and energy to contribute to your life or to make or shop for your gift.

3. **The Impact of the Gift**: Let the giver know what their gift—a physical object, act of service, or shared experience—means to you. For example, how did receiving it make you feel? Did it cheer you up or give you more confidence? How will you use the gift and savor it in your life? What does their gift allow you to do, or what trouble will it help you avoid?

In the space below, list the three aspects of the gift you will be expressing appreciation for. The more specific you can be, the better.

____

____

A final instruction before you take action: As you know, taking the time to actually thank another human being, either verbally or in writing, is wonderful both for the receiver and the giver—*but it must be genuine*. Anything but total authenticity defeats the whole purpose. So find that place of true gratitude and sincere appreciation inside you and continue to the next step.

Step 3: ***Just Do It!***

Right now, go thank the person you selected—either face-to-face, on the phone, in an email or text, or in a written thank-you note sent through the mail—and then come back to the workbook and put a check mark next to their name in Step 1.

Take A Moment to Reflect: How did that feel? In the space below, take a few minutes to write any insights, feelings, or thoughts that came up when you expressed your appreciation in this way:

To make this a habit, the 30-Day Tracker has a space for you to note, each day, the name of someone you'd like to appreciate. If no one comes to mind on a particular day, please come back to this section and choose one of the people you listed.

We also suggest you buy beautiful thank-you notes and postage stamps to keep on hand as expressing appreciation becomes part of your daily experience.

Receiving Appreciation is Important for Luck Too

Receiving appreciation is also an essential part of creating good fortune. Your ability to accept praise and gratitude from others is directly proportional to your capacity to accept more luck in your life.

So, how are you at receiving appreciation? Think of the last time someone thanked you for something you did, or praised your appearance, talent, or character. Did you simply say *thank you* and enjoy the acknowledgment? Or did you deflect, diminish your role, say something self-deprecating, or compliment them back out of your own discomfort?

If receiving appreciation is a challenge for you—and it is for most people, especially women—practice the following exercise.

If you're already comfortable with absorbing appreciation from others, you're ahead of the game! Please do the following exercise anyway, just to be sure there are no hidden glitches in your appreciation-receiving machinery.

Exercise: Receiving Appreciation from Others

Step 1. Close your eyes and imagine someone you care about giving you a compliment or thanking you for something. Notice your reaction. Does the thought make you smile, or squirm? Do your body and breathing expand? Or do they contract?

If you feel uncomfortable in any way, take a few deep belly-breaths and simply be with your feelings, taking note of their intensity. When you feel complete, open your eyes and continue.

- If your discomfort is mild, it's likely just an unfortunate habit that can be overcome with some practice. Continue on to Step 2.
- If you experience severe discomfort, it's probably coming from an Upper Limit Problem (ULP). In this case, we suggest you go back and repeat the ULP exercises found in Chapter 2 to work on any feelings of unworthiness. Then, come back to this exercise and continue.

Step 2. Close your eyes and imagine someone appreciating you with the following phrases, filling in the blanks with something true about you: "Wow, you are so good at __________," or "You did an amazing job of __________," or "You look terrific!" or "Thank you so much for __________." Let these words resonate inside you.

Now, place your hands over your heart and say out loud: *thank you*. Putting your hands over your heart connects you emotionally to what's being said and opens up a space for you to truly receive, rather than deflect, the positive energy coming your way. It's okay if you feel weird or stupid or awkward—just let those feelings be there. Your goal is to make receiving praise and responding with a genuine *thank you* a familiar and natural process.

Next, keeping your eyes closed and your hands over your heart, say *thank you* out loud 10 more times, pausing and taking a slow deep belly-breath after each thank you. It's important to say the words out loud so you become comfortable with this most basic act of receiving.

We suggest you continue practicing Step 2 as often as you can—in the shower, before you go to sleep, or any time and place it feels appropriate to close your eyes and place your hands over your heart.

You can also practice saying *thank you* out loud with your eyes open and without putting your hands on your heart—while cooking, driving, or walking. Keep practicing receiving until you can stay open, smile, look directly at the person appreciating you, and say *thank you* easily when the real thing happens.

Take a Moment to Reflect: How did you feel doing this exercise? If it was uncomfortable for you, why do you think that is? Can you remember any events in your life or any messages you received growing up that might have impacted your ability to accept praise and appreciation? How do feel about the possibility of enjoying saying *thank you*? In the space below, write down any insights, memories, or experiences that came up for you:

____

____

____

____

____

____

It's important to understand that accepting praise doesn't make you boastful or arrogant. It simply allows you to acknowledge how your gifts and abilities are perceived by those around you. If we deflect someone's appreciation, we are essentially rejecting their good opinion of us, rejecting them, and blocking positivity—including more luck—from coming into our lives.

Practicing Radical Gratitude

As you learned in *Conscious Luck*, feeling grateful and feeling lucky are two sides of the same coin; feeling one leads to feeling the other. So, the formula for being luckier is simple: Learn to be more grateful, more often.

Of course, it's easy to be grateful for the positive events in our lives, but what about when you encounter challenging situations? How can you feel grateful then? The answer is by practicing Radical Gratitude, the two-step process we introduced in *Conscious Luck*, which allows you to be grateful for your setbacks as well as your gifts.

Whenever you're faced with an upsetting or stressful event, the first step of this practice asks you to "feel your feelings" about your disappointment, struggle, or challenge—whatever those feelings are. This is vitally important, because too often your desire to be grateful or to "count your blessings" can cause you to suppress and ignore your difficult emotions. Suppression may ease your pain in the short-term, but over time it can impair your capacity to feel your feelings and to empathize with others.

We are not suggesting that you should wallow in or focus indefinitely on your more challenging emotions, but it *is* healthy to be with whatever is real for you. Venting in private for a limited period—for example, through crying, shouting, or journaling—can help you process and move beyond your initial reactions.

Once you've attended to your emotions, the second step of the Radical Gratitude practice requires you to simply ask yourself if there is anything about what happened to you that you could be grateful for, and then listen for the answers. Just being open to a different perspective of the situation immediately releases you from the grip of victimhood.

To apply the practice of Radical Gratitude more easily in your own life, we've created a worksheet for you to use. (A hat-tip to leadership coach David Byrd for the inspiration!)

Exercise: The Radical Gratitude Worksheet

Step 1: On the left-hand side of the following form, take five minutes (or ten minutes maximum) to write out by hand how you feel about a current challenge, disappointment, or setback you're facing in any area of your life. Set a timer so you can focus just on your writing.

Don't hold back. Don't be nice or reasonable or fair. Just let the words flow from your heart onto the page. No one will see it but you.

NOTE: If there's a chance that someone you're writing about could find this book, do this step of the exercise on a separate piece of paper that you can safely burn or shred.

When you finish, go on to Step 2, which is found on the page after the worksheet form.

How do I feel about the situation?	**Is there *anything* about this situation that I could be grateful for?**

Step 2: Take a few belly-breaths and then, on the right-hand side of the same worksheet, answer the question: Is there *anything* about this situation I could be grateful for?

Remember, there is no "should" or obligation to feel grateful—just a gentle curiosity to see what emerges from this line of inquiry. Write anything that surfaces. It's okay if nothing does. Just asking the question and being open to an answer have a powerful effect.

Take a Moment to Reflect: How did this exercise feel for you? Did anything unexpected emerge? Do you feel better about the situation after writing about it? Can you see anything lucky, or potentially lucky, about the circumstance or event? In the space below, write down any thoughts, insights, or experiences you want to remember:

____

____

____

____

____

____

The Radical Gratitude process allows you to find true gratitude that's rooted in your authentic experience. Plus, it's fun to see what amazing, creative ideas surface when you open the door to a larger reality.

Cultivating a Buoyant Spirit

Sometimes, no matter what you do, setbacks remain setbacks. There will be times when you're unable to find a silver lining in your storm clouds. When this happens, the most important thing is to be gentle with yourself: breathe, let your feelings be, and if necessary, call in the support of your lucky community to "hold you" as you heal.

It can also help to sit quietly and look back over your life for other negative or challenging situations that ended up turning out well—or at least better than expected—or which, in time, led to good luck.

With a broader perspective, you can see that the events that caused distress and worry in the past didn't always culminate in the permanent catastrophe you feared. This approach to difficult events is not only comforting; more importantly, it helps you avoid fight-or-flight reactions and use a higher brain function to navigate your way to a better—and luckier—outcome.

Take a Moment to Reflect: Have you experienced an unlucky event that actually paved the way for some wonderful new direction for you? For example:

- Did losing your job free you up to find a better career?
- Was breaking up with someone, though devastating, the prelude to meeting your ideal partner?
- Did a health scare motivate you to adopt healthier habits?
- Did a financial loss lead you to simplify your life and live more happily within your means?

Capture one or two scenarios below. Make sure to include how they benefited you:

____

____

____

____

____

____

Research has shown that unlucky people let adversity shut them down, leading them to make the decision, consciously or unconsciously, to play small in life in order to remain "safe."

Lucky people, on the other hand, are highly resilient, and refuse to allow failure and disappointment to stop them from trying again, from taking risks, or from pursuing new opportunities. Win or lose, they look for the luck in every situation, are grateful when they find it, and then get right back on the horse.

To cultivate that same buoyant spirit, consistently practice Radical Gratitude and learn to take a longer view of current events. Your serenity *and* your luck will grow significantly.

✤

You did it! You completed the "heart" of the workbook! We hope this in-depth exploration of the eight Secrets has brought you a more profound understanding of yourself—and the power you have to intentionally change your fortune.

But don't stop now. Take all you've learned here and apply it in the world out there. Make it a natural part of who you are and how you live. To accomplish this, use the 30-day tracker found in Part 3—not just once, but again and again. Keep practicing and working on your habits until you've established luck at the core of your being.

Keep committing to being lucky.

Keep noticing if you fall into old patterns of behavior so you can gently course correct.

Keep becoming aware of the places you carry shame in your body and breathe light into them.

Keep setting goals that give luck a reason to visit.

Keep stretching yourself and finding the courage to hurl yourself through those windows of opportunity as they arise.

Keep looking for the people who fan your flames and cheer you on, and make them your inner circle.

Keep *really* listening to, feeling connected to, and being your truest self.

Keep radiating appreciation and experiencing as much gratitude as you can during the precious time you have on this amazing planet.

Your lucky life is waiting for you…

PART THREE

Incorporating Luck into Your Daily Life

Keeping Track of Your Progress

For our habits make us, and we make our habits.

—Frederick Langbridge, 19th century writer

Let us introduce you to your new best friends: The 21-Day Luck Activation Journal and the 30-Day Lucky Life Tracker. Think of these pages as your always-available, always-willing-to-help Conscious Luck accountability partners, here to keep you on course as you create luckier habits.

Habits are formed by repeating a behavior over and over until it becomes automatic. This works against you if you let behaviors that create bad luck become your default. But when you consciously choose actions that create good fortune and intentionally practice them, you place yourself on the fast track to luck.

The Eight Secrets of Conscious Luck describe in detail the behaviors, attitudes, and associations required to be luckier. The trackers that follow have been designed to help you create good fortune more effectively in your daily life by reminding you to

- set your intention to be lucky each morning,
- schedule and perform the luck-boosting actions prescribed in the Secrets each day,
- practice gratitude consistently,
- record and celebrate your progress each night, and
- prepare your subconscious mind to absorb your luck-affirmations while you sleep.

We hope you'll take advantage of their enormous power to help you establish lucky habits as your standard operating procedure. Happy tracking!

21-Day Luck Activation Journal

Complete One Page per Day

Using the 21-Day Luck Activation Journal

The 21-Day Luck Activation Journal is to be used as you work your way through Part 2 of this workbook. ***Please start using the Journal as soon as you begin Part 2.***

If it takes you longer than 21 days to complete Part 2, or if you simply find you need additional journal pages, go to www.consciousluck.com/workbook to print off more. If you complete Part 2 in fewer than 21 days, feel free to begin using the 30-Day Lucky Life Tracker, which incorporates the material presented in Part 2.

Instructions

In the morning:

1. Listen to the Morning Conscious Luck Activation Meditation audio recording, or simply close your eyes and repeat—either silently or aloud—the Conscious Luck affirmations listed in that section of the journal page, to reinforce your commitment to being luckier each day.

   If you haven't downloaded the meditation audio recordings yet, please do so at www.consciousluck.com/workbook.

2. Write your Conscious Luck commitment in the space provided. Writing the sentence engages your body, as well as your mind and emotions, in the process of commitment. Daily repetition deepens its impact.

   Both steps 1 and 2 support the first Conscious Luck Secret: *Commit to Be a VLP—A Very Lucky Person.*

3. OPTIONAL: Fill in the Gratitude section. Although it's labeled as an evening activity, you may fill in the gratitude section either in the morning, evening, or both. Review your day for any positive experiences and take a few minutes to consciously enjoy all the good experiences you had. Be sure to vary the things you're grateful for from day to day. This step is based on the eighth Conscious Luck Secret: *Practice Radical Gratitude and Appreciation.*

In the evening:

1. If you haven't filled in the Gratitude section or want to do it twice a day, complete this section at the start of your evening journaling session.

2. Complete the Daily Luck Inventory. Identify at least one—and ideally three—lucky occurrences from your day. Review the day for anything that felt lucky to you: synchronicities, breakthroughs, hoped-for or unexpected successes, or being at the right place at the right time—perhaps finding a parking space, or money in your pocket or on the street.

   There's a limited amount of space in which to write there, so if there's something spectacular you'd like to document more fully, please feel free to use the NOTES section at the very back of the book.

   Doing a luck inventory on a regular basis amplifies your experience of being lucky. Here's how it works:

   > When you repeatedly practice looking for luck, your Reticular Activating System (RAS), the part of your brain that sorts through incoming data for important information, becomes programmed to bring lucky events to your attention so that you recognize and register being lucky more often.
   >
   > As you notice more and more luck, you naturally begin to feel like a lucky person—you expect more luck and are more optimistic overall. This is the hallmark of a lucky mindset.
   >
   > This mindset combined with your increased awareness of lucky events boosts both your luck *and* your perception of it. These feed one another in a classic positive feedback loop, or what we call a "luck spiral"—great motivation to do your luck inventory every day!

3. To end your day, ideally just before falling asleep, listen to the Evening Conscious Luck Activation Meditation audio or simply close your eyes and repeat—silently or aloud—the Conscious Luck affirmations listed in that section of the journal page. This sets you up to absorb the luck messages at a deeper level while you sleep.

Date: ________________

MORNING: **Morning Luck Meditation**: To reinforce your willingness and commitment to being luckier, play the Morning Luck Meditation recording or take three deep belly-breaths and say each of these phrases, silently or out loud, three times:

- Today I am willing to be luckier than I've ever been before.
- I commit to being luckier than I've ever been before.
- Today, I am always in the right place at the right time for good luck to happen to me.

On the lines below, write your commitment, I, ________________, make a sincere commitment to being lucky, now and forever.

____

____

EVENING: What am I grateful for? List as many things as you can:

____

____

Luck Inventory: Record synchronicities, breakthroughs, and right place/right time events—anything that felt lucky. Or simply appreciate your willingness to be lucky.

____

____

Evening Luck Meditation: To help your subconscious absorb luck-attracting concepts while you sleep, play the Evening Meditation recording or take three deep belly-breaths and say each of these phrases to yourself, silently or aloud, three times:

- I AM lucky.
- I deserve to be lucky.
- I see lucky opportunities around me.
- I trust my inner guidance.
- I see luck in every situation.

Now drift off to a lucky slumber.

Date: ________________

MORNING: **Morning Luck Meditation**: To reinforce your willingness and commitment to being luckier, play the Morning Luck Meditation recording or take three deep belly-breaths and say each of these phrases, silently or out loud, three times:

- Today I am willing to be luckier than I've ever been before.
- I commit to being luckier than I've ever been before.
- Today, I am always in the right place at the right time for good luck to happen to me.

On the lines below, write your commitment, I, ________________, make a sincere commitment to being lucky, now and forever.

____

____

EVENING: What am I grateful for? List as many things as you can:

____

____

Luck Inventory: Record synchronicities, breakthroughs, and right place/right time events—anything that felt lucky. Or simply appreciate your willingness to be lucky.

____

____

Evening Luck Meditation: To help your subconscious absorb luck-attracting concepts while you sleep, play the Evening Meditation recording or take three deep belly-breaths and say each of these phrases to yourself, silently or aloud, three times:

- I AM lucky.
- I deserve to be lucky.
- I see lucky opportunities around me.
- I trust my inner guidance.
- I see luck in every situation.

Now drift off to a lucky slumber.

Date: ________________

MORNING: **Morning Luck Meditation**: To reinforce your willingness and commitment to being luckier, play the Morning Luck Meditation recording or take three deep belly-breaths and say each of these phrases, silently or out loud, three times:

- Today I am willing to be luckier than I've ever been before.
- I commit to being luckier than I've ever been before.
- Today, I am always in the right place at the right time for good luck to happen to me.

On the lines below, write your commitment, I, ________________, make a sincere commitment to being lucky, now and forever.

____

____

EVENING: What am I grateful for? List as many things as you can:

____

____

Luck Inventory: Record synchronicities, breakthroughs, and right place/right time events—anything that felt lucky. Or simply appreciate your willingness to be lucky.

____

____

Evening Luck Meditation: To help your subconscious absorb luck-attracting concepts while you sleep, play the Evening Meditation recording or take three deep belly-breaths and say each of these phrases to yourself, silently or aloud, three times:

- I AM lucky.
- I deserve to be lucky.
- I see lucky opportunities around me.
- I trust my inner guidance.
- I see luck in every situation.

Now drift off to a lucky slumber.

Date: ____________________

MORNING: **Morning Luck Meditation**: To reinforce your willingness and commitment to being luckier, play the Morning Luck Meditation recording or take three deep belly-breaths and say each of these phrases, silently or out loud, three times:

- Today I am willing to be luckier than I've ever been before.
- I commit to being luckier than I've ever been before.
- Today, I am always in the right place at the right time for good luck to happen to me.

On the lines below, write your commitment, I, ________________, make a sincere commitment to being lucky, now and forever.

____

____

EVENING: What am I grateful for? List as many things as you can:

____

____

Luck Inventory: Record synchronicities, breakthroughs, and right place/right time events—anything that felt lucky. Or simply appreciate your willingness to be lucky.

____

____

Evening Luck Meditation: To help your subconscious absorb luck-attracting concepts while you sleep, play the Evening Meditation recording or take three deep belly-breaths and say each of these phrases to yourself, silently or aloud, three times:

- I AM lucky.
- I deserve to be lucky.
- I see lucky opportunities around me.
- I trust my inner guidance.
- I see luck in every situation.

Now drift off to a lucky slumber.

Date: ________________

MORNING: **Morning Luck Meditation**: To reinforce your willingness and commitment to being luckier, play the Morning Luck Meditation recording or take three deep belly-breaths and say each of these phrases, silently or out loud, three times:

- Today I am willing to be luckier than I've ever been before.
- I commit to being luckier than I've ever been before.
- Today, I am always in the right place at the right time for good luck to happen to me.

On the lines below, write your commitment, I, ________________, make a sincere commitment to being lucky, now and forever.

____

____

EVENING: What am I grateful for? List as many things as you can:

____

____

Luck Inventory: Record synchronicities, breakthroughs, and right place/right time events—anything that felt lucky. Or simply appreciate your willingness to be lucky.

____

____

Evening Luck Meditation: To help your subconscious absorb luck-attracting concepts while you sleep, play the Evening Meditation recording or take three deep belly-breaths and say each of these phrases to yourself, silently or aloud, three times:

- I AM lucky.
- I deserve to be lucky.
- I see lucky opportunities around me.
- I trust my inner guidance.
- I see luck in every situation.

Now drift off to a lucky slumber.

Date: ________________

MORNING: **Morning Luck Meditation**: To reinforce your willingness and commitment to being luckier, play the Morning Luck Meditation recording or take three deep belly-breaths and say each of these phrases, silently or out loud, three times:

- Today I am willing to be luckier than I've ever been before.
- I commit to being luckier than I've ever been before.
- Today, I am always in the right place at the right time for good luck to happen to me.

On the lines below, write your commitment, I, ________________, make a sincere commitment to being lucky, now and forever.

____

____

EVENING: What am I grateful for? List as many things as you can:

____

____

Luck Inventory: Record synchronicities, breakthroughs, and right place/right time events—anything that felt lucky. Or simply appreciate your willingness to be lucky.

____

____

Evening Luck Meditation: To help your subconscious absorb luck-attracting concepts while you sleep, play the Evening Meditation recording or take three deep belly-breaths and say each of these phrases to yourself, silently or aloud, three times:

- I AM lucky.
- I deserve to be lucky.
- I see lucky opportunities around me.
- I trust my inner guidance.
- I see luck in every situation.

Now drift off to a lucky slumber.

Date: ________________

MORNING: **Morning Luck Meditation**: To reinforce your willingness and commitment to being luckier, play the Morning Luck Meditation recording or take three deep belly-breaths and say each of these phrases, silently or out loud, three times:

- Today I am willing to be luckier than I've ever been before.
- I commit to being luckier than I've ever been before.
- Today, I am always in the right place at the right time for good luck to happen to me.

On the lines below, write your commitment, I, ________________, make a sincere commitment to being lucky, now and forever.

____

____

EVENING: What am I grateful for? List as many things as you can:

____

____

Luck Inventory: Record synchronicities, breakthroughs, and right place/right time events—anything that felt lucky. Or simply appreciate your willingness to be lucky.

____

____

Evening Luck Meditation: To help your subconscious absorb luck-attracting concepts while you sleep, play the Evening Meditation recording or take three deep belly-breaths and say each of these phrases to yourself, silently or aloud, three times:

- I AM lucky.
- I deserve to be lucky.
- I see lucky opportunities around me.
- I trust my inner guidance.
- I see luck in every situation.

Now drift off to a lucky slumber.

Date: ________________

MORNING: **Morning Luck Meditation**: To reinforce your willingness and commitment to being luckier, play the Morning Luck Meditation recording or take three deep belly-breaths and say each of these phrases, silently or out loud, three times:

- Today I am willing to be luckier than I've ever been before.
- I commit to being luckier than I've ever been before.
- Today, I am always in the right place at the right time for good luck to happen to me.

On the lines below, write your commitment, I, ________________, make a sincere commitment to being lucky, now and forever.

____

____

EVENING: What am I grateful for? List as many things as you can:

____

____

Luck Inventory: Record synchronicities, breakthroughs, and right place/right time events—anything that felt lucky. Or simply appreciate your willingness to be lucky.

____

____

Evening Luck Meditation: To help your subconscious absorb luck-attracting concepts while you sleep, play the Evening Meditation recording or take three deep belly-breaths and say each of these phrases to yourself, silently or aloud, three times:

- I AM lucky.
- I deserve to be lucky.
- I see lucky opportunities around me.
- I trust my inner guidance.
- I see luck in every situation.

Now drift off to a lucky slumber.

Date: ________________

MORNING: **Morning Luck Meditation**: To reinforce your willingness and commitment to being luckier, play the Morning Luck Meditation recording or take three deep belly-breaths and say each of these phrases, silently or out loud, three times:

- Today I am willing to be luckier than I've ever been before.
- I commit to being luckier than I've ever been before.
- Today, I am always in the right place at the right time for good luck to happen to me.

On the lines below, write your commitment, I, ________________, make a sincere commitment to being lucky, now and forever.

____

____

EVENING: What am I grateful for? List as many things as you can:

____

____

Luck Inventory: Record synchronicities, breakthroughs, and right place/right time events—anything that felt lucky. Or simply appreciate your willingness to be lucky.

____

____

Evening Luck Meditation: To help your subconscious absorb luck-attracting concepts while you sleep, play the Evening Meditation recording or take three deep belly-breaths and say each of these phrases to yourself, silently or aloud, three times:

- I AM lucky.
- I deserve to be lucky.
- I see lucky opportunities around me.
- I trust my inner guidance.
- I see luck in every situation.

Now drift off to a lucky slumber.

Date: ________________

MORNING: **Morning Luck Meditation**: To reinforce your willingness and commitment to being luckier, play the Morning Luck Meditation recording or take three deep belly-breaths and say each of these phrases, silently or out loud, three times:

- Today I am willing to be luckier than I've ever been before.
- I commit to being luckier than I've ever been before.
- Today, I am always in the right place at the right time for good luck to happen to me.

On the lines below, write your commitment, I, ________________, make a sincere commitment to being lucky, now and forever.

____

____

EVENING: What am I grateful for? List as many things as you can:

____

____

Luck Inventory: Record synchronicities, breakthroughs, and right place/right time events—anything that felt lucky. Or simply appreciate your willingness to be lucky.

____

____

Evening Luck Meditation: To help your subconscious absorb luck-attracting concepts while you sleep, play the Evening Meditation recording or take three deep belly-breaths and say each of these phrases to yourself, silently or aloud, three times:

- I AM lucky.
- I deserve to be lucky.
- I see lucky opportunities around me.
- I trust my inner guidance.
- I see luck in every situation.

Now drift off to a lucky slumber.

Date: ________________

MORNING: **Morning Luck Meditation**: To reinforce your willingness and commitment to being luckier, play the Morning Luck Meditation recording or take three deep belly-breaths and say each of these phrases, silently or out loud, three times:

- Today I am willing to be luckier than I've ever been before.
- I commit to being luckier than I've ever been before.
- Today, I am always in the right place at the right time for good luck to happen to me.

On the lines below, write your commitment, I, ________________, make a sincere commitment to being lucky, now and forever.

____

____

EVENING: What am I grateful for? List as many things as you can:

____

____

Luck Inventory: Record synchronicities, breakthroughs, and right place/right time events—anything that felt lucky. Or simply appreciate your willingness to be lucky.

____

____

Evening Luck Meditation: To help your subconscious absorb luck-attracting concepts while you sleep, play the Evening Meditation recording or take three deep belly-breaths and say each of these phrases to yourself, silently or aloud, three times:

- I AM lucky.
- I deserve to be lucky.
- I see lucky opportunities around me.
- I trust my inner guidance.
- I see luck in every situation.

Now drift off to a lucky slumber.

Date: ________________

MORNING: **Morning Luck Meditation**: To reinforce your willingness and commitment to being luckier, play the Morning Luck Meditation recording or take three deep belly-breaths and say each of these phrases, silently or out loud, three times:

- Today I am willing to be luckier than I've ever been before.
- I commit to being luckier than I've ever been before.
- Today, I am always in the right place at the right time for good luck to happen to me.

On the lines below, write your commitment, I, ______________, make a sincere commitment to being lucky, now and forever.

____

____

EVENING: What am I grateful for? List as many things as you can:

____

____

Luck Inventory: Record synchronicities, breakthroughs, and right place/right time events—anything that felt lucky. Or simply appreciate your willingness to be lucky.

____

____

Evening Luck Meditation: To help your subconscious absorb luck-attracting concepts while you sleep, play the Evening Meditation recording or take three deep belly-breaths and say each of these phrases to yourself, silently or aloud, three times:

- I AM lucky.
- I deserve to be lucky.
- I see lucky opportunities around me.
- I trust my inner guidance.
- I see luck in every situation.

Now drift off to a lucky slumber.

Date: ________________

MORNING: **Morning Luck Meditation**: To reinforce your willingness and commitment to being luckier, play the Morning Luck Meditation recording or take three deep belly-breaths and say each of these phrases, silently or out loud, three times:

- Today I am willing to be luckier than I've ever been before.
- I commit to being luckier than I've ever been before.
- Today, I am always in the right place at the right time for good luck to happen to me.

On the lines below, write your commitment, I, ________________, make a sincere commitment to being lucky, now and forever.

____

____

EVENING: What am I grateful for? List as many things as you can:

____

____

Luck Inventory: Record synchronicities, breakthroughs, and right place/right time events—anything that felt lucky. Or simply appreciate your willingness to be lucky.

____

____

Evening Luck Meditation: To help your subconscious absorb luck-attracting concepts while you sleep, play the Evening Meditation recording or take three deep belly-breaths and say each of these phrases to yourself, silently or aloud, three times:

- I AM lucky.
- I deserve to be lucky.
- I see lucky opportunities around me.
- I trust my inner guidance.
- I see luck in every situation.

Now drift off to a lucky slumber.

Date: ________________

MORNING: **Morning Luck Meditation**: To reinforce your willingness and commitment to being luckier, play the Morning Luck Meditation recording or take three deep belly-breaths and say each of these phrases, silently or out loud, three times:

- Today I am willing to be luckier than I've ever been before.
- I commit to being luckier than I've ever been before.
- Today, I am always in the right place at the right time for good luck to happen to me.

On the lines below, write your commitment, I, ________________, make a sincere commitment to being lucky, now and forever.

____

____

EVENING: What am I grateful for? List as many things as you can:

____

____

Luck Inventory: Record synchronicities, breakthroughs, and right place/right time events—anything that felt lucky. Or simply appreciate your willingness to be lucky.

____

____

Evening Luck Meditation: To help your subconscious absorb luck-attracting concepts while you sleep, play the Evening Meditation recording or take three deep belly-breaths and say each of these phrases to yourself, silently or aloud, three times:

- I AM lucky.
- I deserve to be lucky.
- I see lucky opportunities around me.
- I trust my inner guidance.
- I see luck in every situation.

Now drift off to a lucky slumber.

Date: ________________

MORNING: **Morning Luck Meditation**: To reinforce your willingness and commitment to being luckier, play the Morning Luck Meditation recording or take three deep belly-breaths and say each of these phrases, silently or out loud, three times:

- Today I am willing to be luckier than I've ever been before.
- I commit to being luckier than I've ever been before.
- Today, I am always in the right place at the right time for good luck to happen to me.

On the lines below, write your commitment, I, ________________, make a sincere commitment to being lucky, now and forever.

____

____

EVENING: What am I grateful for? List as many things as you can:

____

____

Luck Inventory: Record synchronicities, breakthroughs, and right place/right time events—anything that felt lucky. Or simply appreciate your willingness to be lucky.

____

____

Evening Luck Meditation: To help your subconscious absorb luck-attracting concepts while you sleep, play the Evening Meditation recording or take three deep belly-breaths and say each of these phrases to yourself, silently or aloud, three times:

- I AM lucky.
- I deserve to be lucky.
- I see lucky opportunities around me.
- I trust my inner guidance.
- I see luck in every situation.

Now drift off to a lucky slumber.

Date: ________________

MORNING: **Morning Luck Meditation**: To reinforce your willingness and commitment to being luckier, play the Morning Luck Meditation recording or take three deep belly-breaths and say each of these phrases, silently or out loud, three times:

- Today I am willing to be luckier than I've ever been before.
- I commit to being luckier than I've ever been before.
- Today, I am always in the right place at the right time for good luck to happen to me.

On the lines below, write your commitment, I, ________________, make a sincere commitment to being lucky, now and forever.

____

____

EVENING: What am I grateful for? List as many things as you can:

____

____

Luck Inventory: Record synchronicities, breakthroughs, and right place/right time events—anything that felt lucky. Or simply appreciate your willingness to be lucky.

____

____

Evening Luck Meditation: To help your subconscious absorb luck-attracting concepts while you sleep, play the Evening Meditation recording or take three deep belly-breaths and say each of these phrases to yourself, silently or aloud, three times:

- I AM lucky.
- I deserve to be lucky.
- I see lucky opportunities around me.
- I trust my inner guidance.
- I see luck in every situation.

Now drift off to a lucky slumber.

Date: ________________

MORNING: **Morning Luck Meditation**: To reinforce your willingness and commitment to being luckier, play the Morning Luck Meditation recording or take three deep belly-breaths and say each of these phrases, silently or out loud, three times:

- Today I am willing to be luckier than I've ever been before.
- I commit to being luckier than I've ever been before.
- Today, I am always in the right place at the right time for good luck to happen to me.

On the lines below, write your commitment, I, ________________, make a sincere commitment to being lucky, now and forever.

____

____

EVENING: What am I grateful for? List as many things as you can:

____

____

Luck Inventory: Record synchronicities, breakthroughs, and right place/right time events—anything that felt lucky. Or simply appreciate your willingness to be lucky.

____

____

Evening Luck Meditation: To help your subconscious absorb luck-attracting concepts while you sleep, play the Evening Meditation recording or take three deep belly-breaths and say each of these phrases to yourself, silently or aloud, three times:

- I AM lucky.
- I deserve to be lucky.
- I see lucky opportunities around me.
- I trust my inner guidance.
- I see luck in every situation.

Now drift off to a lucky slumber.

Date: ________________

MORNING: **Morning Luck Meditation**: To reinforce your willingness and commitment to being luckier, play the Morning Luck Meditation recording or take three deep belly-breaths and say each of these phrases, silently or out loud, three times:

- Today I am willing to be luckier than I've ever been before.
- I commit to being luckier than I've ever been before.
- Today, I am always in the right place at the right time for good luck to happen to me.

On the lines below, write your commitment, I, ______________, make a sincere commitment to being lucky, now and forever.

____

____

EVENING: What am I grateful for? List as many things as you can:

____

____

Luck Inventory: Record synchronicities, breakthroughs, and right place/right time events—anything that felt lucky. Or simply appreciate your willingness to be lucky.

____

____

Evening Luck Meditation: To help your subconscious absorb luck-attracting concepts while you sleep, play the Evening Meditation recording or take three deep belly-breaths and say each of these phrases to yourself, silently or aloud, three times:

- I AM lucky.
- I deserve to be lucky.
- I see lucky opportunities around me.
- I trust my inner guidance.
- I see luck in every situation.

Now drift off to a lucky slumber.

Date: ________________

MORNING: **Morning Luck Meditation**: To reinforce your willingness and commitment to being luckier, play the Morning Luck Meditation recording or take three deep belly-breaths and say each of these phrases, silently or out loud, three times:

- Today I am willing to be luckier than I've ever been before.
- I commit to being luckier than I've ever been before.
- Today, I am always in the right place at the right time for good luck to happen to me.

On the lines below, write your commitment, I, ________________, make a sincere commitment to being lucky, now and forever.

____

____

EVENING: What am I grateful for? List as many things as you can:

____

____

Luck Inventory: Record synchronicities, breakthroughs, and right place/right time events—anything that felt lucky. Or simply appreciate your willingness to be lucky.

____

____

Evening Luck Meditation: To help your subconscious absorb luck-attracting concepts while you sleep, play the Evening Meditation recording or take three deep belly-breaths and say each of these phrases to yourself, silently or aloud, three times:

- I AM lucky.
- I deserve to be lucky.
- I see lucky opportunities around me.
- I trust my inner guidance.
- I see luck in every situation.

Now drift off to a lucky slumber.

Date: ________________

MORNING: **Morning Luck Meditation**: To reinforce your willingness and commitment to being luckier, play the Morning Luck Meditation recording or take three deep belly-breaths and say each of these phrases, silently or out loud, three times:

- Today I am willing to be luckier than I've ever been before.
- I commit to being luckier than I've ever been before.
- Today, I am always in the right place at the right time for good luck to happen to me.

On the lines below, write your commitment, I, ________________, make a sincere commitment to being lucky, now and forever.

____

____

EVENING: What am I grateful for? List as many things as you can:

____

____

Luck Inventory: Record synchronicities, breakthroughs, and right place/right time events—anything that felt lucky. Or simply appreciate your willingness to be lucky.

____

____

Evening Luck Meditation: To help your subconscious absorb luck-attracting concepts while you sleep, play the Evening Meditation recording or take three deep belly-breaths and say each of these phrases to yourself, silently or aloud, three times:

- I AM lucky.
- I deserve to be lucky.
- I see lucky opportunities around me.
- I trust my inner guidance.
- I see luck in every situation.

Now drift off to a lucky slumber.

Date: ________________

MORNING: **Morning Luck Meditation**: To reinforce your willingness and commitment to being luckier, play the Morning Luck Meditation recording or take three deep belly-breaths and say each of these phrases, silently or out loud, three times:

- Today I am willing to be luckier than I've ever been before.
- I commit to being luckier than I've ever been before.
- Today, I am always in the right place at the right time for good luck to happen to me.

On the lines below, write your commitment, I, ________________, make a sincere commitment to being lucky, now and forever.

____

____

EVENING: What am I grateful for? List as many things as you can:

____

____

Luck Inventory: Record synchronicities, breakthroughs, and right place/right time events—anything that felt lucky. Or simply appreciate your willingness to be lucky.

____

____

Evening Luck Meditation: To help your subconscious absorb luck-attracting concepts while you sleep, play the Evening Meditation recording or take three deep belly-breaths and say each of these phrases to yourself, silently or aloud, three times:

- I AM lucky.
- I deserve to be lucky.
- I see lucky opportunities around me.
- I trust my inner guidance.
- I see luck in every situation.

Now drift off to a lucky slumber.

30-Day Lucky Life Tracker

Complete Two Pages Per Day:
One in the Morning and One in the Evening

Using the 30-Day Lucky Life Tracker

The 30-Day Lucky Life Tracker is to be used *after* you've completed Part 2. ***As soon as you finish Part 2, please begin using the 30-Day Tracker.***

If you need more pages or want to continue using the tracker after you finish the first 30 days, visit www.consciousluck.com/workbook to download and print additional pages.

Instructions

The Morning Tracker Page sets your Conscious Luck intentions for the day.

1. Listen to the Morning Conscious Luck Activation Meditation audio or repeat the affirmations to yourself, either silently or out loud.
2. Write your Conscious Luck commitment.
3. List the specific action steps you'll work on that day to help you accomplish your selected 30-day goal—either an urgent goal or a sub-goal of a longer-term life goal.

   You can also pick a personal luckifying activity to schedule in if you'd like. Go to the list of action steps you created in Chapter 4 and select at least one for each day. This harnesses the luck-attracting power of the fourth Conscious Luck Secret: *Have Luck-Worthy Goals.*
4. Write down the specific ways you'll mix up your routine today, for example: using a different hand for routine tasks, driving or walking a new route, wearing something unusual for you, or trying a new cuisine. Refer to the list you created in Chapter 5 or come up with some new possibilities.
5. Write the specific bold actions you'll take to get out of your comfort zone as you work toward your goals. Choose from the list you created in Chapter 5 or brainstorm some new ways to use your "20 seconds of insane courage."

   NOTE: Steps 4 and 5 allow you to apply the fifth Conscious Luck Secret: *Take Bold Action Consistently.*

6. The Morning Tracker Page concludes with a gratitude session. Select at least three people, events, situations, or gifts you've received for which you feel grateful. Be thoughtful about what you select and make a point to vary the things you are grateful for each day.

   The *energy* of feeling grateful magnetizes more to be grateful for. So, in addition to listing the things you're grateful for in your life, be sure to take time to savor them fully—this allows your gratitude to register more completely and intensifies the "grateful energy" you feel.

   Doing this session in the morning sends you into your day radiant with positivity and primed to attract luck.

The Evening Tracker Page allows you to reflect on your day and your experiences doing the Conscious Luck practices.

1. Do a Luck Inventory, reviewing the day for lucky occurrences.
2. Track the ways you listened to your inner GPS (applying the seventh Conscious Luck Secret: *Learn to Be at the Right Place at the Right Time*).
   - In what ways did you follow your intuition? By acting on hunches or listening to the still, small voice inside?
   - Did you take time during the day to connect to your essence pace while moving or stationary?
   - How were you guided by your values? Did you check in with your deeper sense of self before making an important decision or stand up for an ethical standard that's important to you?

   The more you use your GPS, the easier and more natural it becomes to receive its messages.
3. Record how you connected to others who inspire and encourage you to be luckier (applying the sixth Conscious Luck Secret: *Find Your Lucky Community*).
   - Did you interact with them, virtually or otherwise?
   - Did you talk to or text your accountability partner, or meet with your mastermind group?

- Did you read 5–10 pages of a personal development book or listen to a personal growth recording or podcast?
- Did you post or comment on the Conscious Luck Global Facebook page?

   If you connected in some other way, there's a blank line for you to fill in. Place a check mark next to all that apply.

4. Catalog the people you expressed appreciation to and how you did so: in person, by email, phone, social media, or text, or by snail mail. If you haven't expressed appreciation yet, catalog how you plan to soon. (The eighth Conscious Luck Secret again!)
5. Review the next day's events on your calendar. Then, take a few minutes to imagine the lucky outcomes you'd like to experience in relation to those events and write them down.

   Doing this before you go to bed will allow those imagined outcomes to "marinate" in your awareness overnight as you sleep. This process programs your subconscious mind and your brain's RAS to be on high alert the next day for anything that could help create those outcomes. As you go through the day, be especially attentive to any hunches, insights, or opportunities that arise, and take action . . . then watch the magic happen!
6. Listen to the Evening Conscious Luck Activation Meditation audio or repeat the affirmations to yourself, either silently or out loud.

A Special Bonus for You

The point of using the trackers is to keep you practicing the Conscious Luck Secrets long enough for you to see results. Your own experience of becoming luckier will be a powerful incentive to continue. Eventually, the attitudes and behaviors you're cultivating will become second nature to you and good luck will be automatic.

In the meantime, to supercharge your motivation, we've created some gifts for you to claim after you've used the 30-Day Tracker for a minimum of 27 days. We'll be relying on the honor system—you won't be sharing your journal pages with us.

Once you have completed at least 27 - 30 days of the Lucky Life Tracker, go to www.consciousluck.com/goalachievement. There you'll find some special bonuses, including access to Q&A calls and other goodies to acknowledge your wins and encourage you to choose another 30-day goal.

Day ________ **Date:** ________________

Luck Tracker: ***MORNING***

1. **Morning Luck Meditation**: To reinforce your willingness and commitment to being luckier, play the Conscious Luck Morning Activation Meditation recording or take three deep belly-breaths and say each of these phrases to yourself three times, silently or out loud:
   - Today I am willing to be luckier than I've ever been before.
   - I commit to being luckier than I've ever been before.
   - Today, I am always in the right place at the right time for good luck to happen to me.

2. Write your commitment below: I, ________________, make a sincere commitment to being lucky, now and forever.

____

____

3. The action steps for my 30-day Goal that I am focusing on today are:

____

____

4. I will mix up my routine today by doing the following activities (if necessary, review your list at the beginning of Chapter 5):

____

____

5. The Bold Actions I will take today toward my Luck-Worthy Goal(s) are:

____

____

6. To attract greater luck to myself, I will start my day full of gratitude. Three things I am grateful for in my life are:

____

____

Luck Tracker: *EVENING*

1. Luck Inventory: Record synchronicities, breakthroughs, right place/right time events—anything that felt lucky. Or simply appreciate your willingness to be lucky.

____

____

2. How did I use my inner GPS today? Did I access my intuition, connect to my essence pace, or feel guided by my values? Write down any instances below:

____

____

3. How did I connect with my lucky community today? Check mark one or more.
   - Via interaction (virtual or otherwise) or by posting on a group FB page
   - By talking to or texting my accountability partner or mastermind group
   - By reading 5–10 pages of a book or listening to a podcast
   - ____

4. Who can I/did I appreciate today, and how? (email, text, in person, mail, or phone)

____

5. Review your calendar for tomorrow and write the lucky outcomes you desire:

____

____

____

6. **Evening Luck Meditation:** To help your subconscious absorb luck-attracting concepts while you sleep, play the Evening Meditation recording or take three deep belly-breaths and say each of these phrases to yourself, silently or aloud, three times:
   - I AM lucky.
   - I deserve to be lucky.
   - I see lucky opportunities around me.
   - I trust my inner guidance.
   - I see luck in every situation.

Now drift off to a lucky slumber.

Day ________ **Date:** ________________

Luck Tracker: ***MORNING***

1. **Morning Luck Meditation**: To reinforce your willingness and commitment to being luckier, play the Conscious Luck Morning Activation Meditation recording or take three deep belly-breaths and say each of these phrases to yourself three times, silently or out loud:
   - Today I am willing to be luckier than I've ever been before.
   - I commit to being luckier than I've ever been before.
   - Today, I am always in the right place at the right time for good luck to happen to me.

2. Write your commitment below: I, ________________, make a sincere commitment to being lucky, now and forever.

____

____

3. The action steps for my 30-day Goal that I am focusing on today are:

____

____

4. I will mix up my routine today by doing the following activities (if necessary, review your list at the beginning of Chapter 5):

____

____

5. The Bold Actions I will take today toward my Luck-Worthy Goal(s) are:

____

____

6. To attract greater luck to myself, I will start my day full of gratitude. Three things I am grateful for in my life are:

____

____

Luck Tracker: ***EVENING***

1. Luck Inventory: Record synchronicities, breakthroughs, right place/right time events—anything that felt lucky. Or simply appreciate your willingness to be lucky.

___

___

2. How did I use my inner GPS today? Did I access my intuition, connect to my essence pace, or feel guided by my values? Write down any instances below:

___

___

3. How did I connect with my lucky community today? Check mark one or more.
   - Via interaction (virtual or otherwise) or by posting on a group FB page
   - By talking to or texting my accountability partner or mastermind group
   - By reading 5–10 pages of a book or listening to a podcast
   - ___

4. Who can I/did I appreciate today, and how? (email, text, in person, mail, or phone)

___

5. Review your calendar for tomorrow and write the lucky outcomes you desire:

___

___

___

6. **Evening Luck Meditation:** To help your subconscious absorb luck-attracting concepts while you sleep, play the Evening Meditation recording or take three deep belly-breaths and say each of these phrases to yourself, silently or aloud, three times:
   - I AM lucky.
   - I deserve to be lucky.
   - I see lucky opportunities around me.
   - I trust my inner guidance.
   - I see luck in every situation.

Now drift off to a lucky slumber.

Day ________ **Date:** ________________

Luck Tracker: ***MORNING***

1. **Morning Luck Meditation**: To reinforce your willingness and commitment to being luckier, play the Conscious Luck Morning Activation Meditation recording or take three deep belly-breaths and say each of these phrases to yourself three times, silently or out loud:
   - Today I am willing to be luckier than I've ever been before.
   - I commit to being luckier than I've ever been before.
   - Today, I am always in the right place at the right time for good luck to happen to me.

2. Write your commitment below: I, ________________, make a sincere commitment to being lucky, now and forever.

____

____

3. The action steps for my 30-day Goal that I am focusing on today are:

____

____

4. I will mix up my routine today by doing the following activities (if necessary, review your list at the beginning of Chapter 5):

____

____

5. The Bold Actions I will take today toward my Luck-Worthy Goal(s) are:

____

____

6. To attract greater luck to myself, I will start my day full of gratitude. Three things I am grateful for in my life are:

____

____

Luck Tracker: *EVENING*

1. Luck Inventory: Record synchronicities, breakthroughs, right place/right time events—anything that felt lucky. Or simply appreciate your willingness to be lucky.

____

____

2. How did I use my inner GPS today? Did I access my intuition, connect to my essence pace, or feel guided by my values? Write down any instances below:

____

____

3. How did I connect with my lucky community today? Check mark one or more.
    - Via interaction (virtual or otherwise) or by posting on a group FB page
    - By talking to or texting my accountability partner or mastermind group
    - By reading 5–10 pages of a book or listening to a podcast
    - ____

4. Who can I/did I appreciate today, and how? (email, text, in person, mail, or phone)

____

5. Review your calendar for tomorrow and write the lucky outcomes you desire:

____

____

____

6. **Evening Luck Meditation:** To help your subconscious absorb luck-attracting concepts while you sleep, play the Evening Meditation recording or take three deep belly-breaths and say each of these phrases to yourself, silently or aloud, three times:
    - I AM lucky.
    - I deserve to be lucky.
    - I see lucky opportunities around me.
    - I trust my inner guidance.
    - I see luck in every situation.

Now drift off to a lucky slumber.

Day ________ **Date:** __________________

Luck Tracker: ***MORNING***

1. **Morning Luck Meditation**: To reinforce your willingness and commitment to being luckier, play the Conscious Luck Morning Activation Meditation recording or take three deep belly-breaths and say each of these phrases to yourself three times, silently or out loud:
   - Today I am willing to be luckier than I've ever been before.
   - I commit to being luckier than I've ever been before.
   - Today, I am always in the right place at the right time for good luck to happen to me.

2. Write your commitment below: I, __________________, make a sincere commitment to being lucky, now and forever.

____

____

3. The action steps for my 30-day Goal that I am focusing on today are:

____

____

4. I will mix up my routine today by doing the following activities (if necessary, review your list at the beginning of Chapter 5):

____

____

5. The Bold Actions I will take today toward my Luck-Worthy Goal(s) are:

____

____

6. To attract greater luck to myself, I will start my day full of gratitude. Three things I am grateful for in my life are:

____

____

Luck Tracker: *EVENING*

1. Luck Inventory: Record synchronicities, breakthroughs, right place/right time events—anything that felt lucky. Or simply appreciate your willingness to be lucky.

____

____

2. How did I use my inner GPS today? Did I access my intuition, connect to my essence pace, or feel guided by my values? Write down any instances below:

____

____

3. How did I connect with my lucky community today? Check mark one or more.
    - Via interaction (virtual or otherwise) or by posting on a group FB page
    - By talking to or texting my accountability partner or mastermind group
    - By reading 5–10 pages of a book or listening to a podcast
    - ____

4. Who can I/did I appreciate today, and how? (email, text, in person, mail, or phone)

____

5. Review your calendar for tomorrow and write the lucky outcomes you desire:

____

____

____

6. **Evening Luck Meditation:** To help your subconscious absorb luck-attracting concepts while you sleep, play the Evening Meditation recording or take three deep belly-breaths and say each of these phrases to yourself, silently or aloud, three times:
    - I AM lucky.
    - I deserve to be lucky.
    - I see lucky opportunities around me.
    - I trust my inner guidance.
    - I see luck in every situation.

Now drift off to a lucky slumber.

Day ________ **Date:** ________________

Luck Tracker: ***MORNING***

1. **Morning Luck Meditation**: To reinforce your willingness and commitment to being luckier, play the Conscious Luck Morning Activation Meditation recording or take three deep belly-breaths and say each of these phrases to yourself three times, silently or out loud:
   - Today I am willing to be luckier than I've ever been before.
   - I commit to being luckier than I've ever been before.
   - Today, I am always in the right place at the right time for good luck to happen to me.
2. Write your commitment below: I, ________________, make a sincere commitment to being lucky, now and forever.

____

____

3. The action steps for my 30-day Goal that I am focusing on today are:

____

____

4. I will mix up my routine today by doing the following activities (if necessary, review your list at the beginning of Chapter 5):

____

____

5. The Bold Actions I will take today toward my Luck-Worthy Goal(s) are:

____

____

6. To attract greater luck to myself, I will start my day full of gratitude. Three things I am grateful for in my life are:

____

____

Luck Tracker: *EVENING*

1. Luck Inventory: Record synchronicities, breakthroughs, right place/right time events—anything that felt lucky. Or simply appreciate your willingness to be lucky.

____

____

2. How did I use my inner GPS today? Did I access my intuition, connect to my essence pace, or feel guided by my values? Write down any instances below:

____

____

3. How did I connect with my lucky community today? Check mark one or more.
   - Via interaction (virtual or otherwise) or by posting on a group FB page
   - By talking to or texting my accountability partner or mastermind group
   - By reading 5–10 pages of a book or listening to a podcast
   - ____

4. Who can I/did I appreciate today, and how? (email, text, in person, mail, or phone)

____

5. Review your calendar for tomorrow and write the lucky outcomes you desire:

____

____

____

6. **Evening Luck Meditation:** To help your subconscious absorb luck-attracting concepts while you sleep, play the Evening Meditation recording or take three deep belly-breaths and say each of these phrases to yourself, silently or aloud, three times:
   - I AM lucky.
   - I deserve to be lucky.
   - I see lucky opportunities around me.
   - I trust my inner guidance.
   - I see luck in every situation.

Now drift off to a lucky slumber.

Day ________ **Date:** ________________

Luck Tracker: ***MORNING***

1. **Morning Luck Meditation**: To reinforce your willingness and commitment to being luckier, play the Conscious Luck Morning Activation Meditation recording or take three deep belly-breaths and say each of these phrases to yourself three times, silently or out loud:
   - Today I am willing to be luckier than I've ever been before.
   - I commit to being luckier than I've ever been before.
   - Today, I am always in the right place at the right time for good luck to happen to me.

2. Write your commitment below: I, ________________, make a sincere commitment to being lucky, now and forever.

____

____

3. The action steps for my 30-day Goal that I am focusing on today are:

____

____

4. I will mix up my routine today by doing the following activities (if necessary, review your list at the beginning of Chapter 5):

____

____

5. The Bold Actions I will take today toward my Luck-Worthy Goal(s) are:

____

____

6. To attract greater luck to myself, I will start my day full of gratitude. Three things I am grateful for in my life are:

____

____

Luck Tracker: *EVENING*

1. Luck Inventory: Record synchronicities, breakthroughs, right place/right time events—anything that felt lucky. Or simply appreciate your willingness to be lucky.

____

____

2. How did I use my inner GPS today? Did I access my intuition, connect to my essence pace, or feel guided by my values? Write down any instances below:

____

____

3. How did I connect with my lucky community today? Check mark one or more.
    - Via interaction (virtual or otherwise) or by posting on a group FB page
    - By talking to or texting my accountability partner or mastermind group
    - By reading 5–10 pages of a book or listening to a podcast
    - ____

4. Who can I/did I appreciate today, and how? (email, text, in person, mail, or phone)

____

5. Review your calendar for tomorrow and write the lucky outcomes you desire:

____

____

____

6. **Evening Luck Meditation:** To help your subconscious absorb luck-attracting concepts while you sleep, play the Evening Meditation recording or take three deep belly-breaths and say each of these phrases to yourself, silently or aloud, three times:
    - I AM lucky.
    - I deserve to be lucky.
    - I see lucky opportunities around me.
    - I trust my inner guidance.
    - I see luck in every situation.

Now drift off to a lucky slumber.

Day ________ **Date:** ________________

Luck Tracker: ***MORNING***

1. **Morning Luck Meditation**: To reinforce your willingness and commitment to being luckier, play the Conscious Luck Morning Activation Meditation recording or take three deep belly-breaths and say each of these phrases to yourself three times, silently or out loud:
   - Today I am willing to be luckier than I've ever been before.
   - I commit to being luckier than I've ever been before.
   - Today, I am always in the right place at the right time for good luck to happen to me.

2. Write your commitment below: I, ________________, make a sincere commitment to being lucky, now and forever.

____

____

3. The action steps for my 30-day Goal that I am focusing on today are:

____

____

4. I will mix up my routine today by doing the following activities (if necessary, review your list at the beginning of Chapter 5):

____

____

5. The Bold Actions I will take today toward my Luck-Worthy Goal(s) are:

____

____

6. To attract greater luck to myself, I will start my day full of gratitude. Three things I am grateful for in my life are:

____

____

Luck Tracker: *EVENING*

1. Luck Inventory: Record synchronicities, breakthroughs, right place/right time events—anything that felt lucky. Or simply appreciate your willingness to be lucky.

____

____

2. How did I use my inner GPS today? Did I access my intuition, connect to my essence pace, or feel guided by my values? Write down any instances below:

____

____

3. How did I connect with my lucky community today? Check mark one or more.
   - Via interaction (virtual or otherwise) or by posting on a group FB page
   - By talking to or texting my accountability partner or mastermind group
   - By reading 5–10 pages of a book or listening to a podcast
   - ______________________________

4. Who can I/did I appreciate today, and how? (email, text, in person, mail, or phone)

____

5. Review your calendar for tomorrow and write the lucky outcomes you desire:

____

____

____

6. **Evening Luck Meditation:** To help your subconscious absorb luck-attracting concepts while you sleep, play the Evening Meditation recording or take three deep belly-breaths and say each of these phrases to yourself, silently or aloud, three times:
   - I AM lucky.
   - I deserve to be lucky.
   - I see lucky opportunities around me.
   - I trust my inner guidance.
   - I see luck in every situation.

Now drift off to a lucky slumber.

Day ________ **Date:** __________________

Luck Tracker: ***MORNING***

1. **Morning Luck Meditation**: To reinforce your willingness and commitment to being luckier, play the Conscious Luck Morning Activation Meditation recording or take three deep belly-breaths and say each of these phrases to yourself three times, silently or out loud:
   - Today I am willing to be luckier than I've ever been before.
   - I commit to being luckier than I've ever been before.
   - Today, I am always in the right place at the right time for good luck to happen to me.

2. Write your commitment below: I, __________________, make a sincere commitment to being lucky, now and forever.

____

____

3. The action steps for my 30-day Goal that I am focusing on today are:

____

____

4. I will mix up my routine today by doing the following activities (if necessary, review your list at the beginning of Chapter 5):

____

____

5. The Bold Actions I will take today toward my Luck-Worthy Goal(s) are:

____

____

6. To attract greater luck to myself, I will start my day full of gratitude. Three things I am grateful for in my life are:

____

____

Luck Tracker: ***EVENING***

1. Luck Inventory: Record synchronicities, breakthroughs, right place/right time events—anything that felt lucky. Or simply appreciate your willingness to be lucky.

____

____

2. How did I use my inner GPS today? Did I access my intuition, connect to my essence pace, or feel guided by my values? Write down any instances below:

____

____

3. How did I connect with my lucky community today? Check mark one or more.
   - Via interaction (virtual or otherwise) or by posting on a group FB page
   - By talking to or texting my accountability partner or mastermind group
   - By reading 5–10 pages of a book or listening to a podcast
   - ______________________________

4. Who can I/did I appreciate today, and how? (email, text, in person, mail, or phone)

____

5. Review your calendar for tomorrow and write the lucky outcomes you desire:

____

____

____

6. **Evening Luck Meditation:** To help your subconscious absorb luck-attracting concepts while you sleep, play the Evening Meditation recording or take three deep belly-breaths and say each of these phrases to yourself, silently or aloud, three times:
   - I AM lucky.
   - I deserve to be lucky.
   - I see lucky opportunities around me.
   - I trust my inner guidance.
   - I see luck in every situation.

Now drift off to a lucky slumber.

Day ________ **Date:** ________________

Luck Tracker: ***MORNING***

1. **Morning Luck Meditation**: To reinforce your willingness and commitment to being luckier, play the Conscious Luck Morning Activation Meditation recording or take three deep belly-breaths and say each of these phrases to yourself three times, silently or out loud:
   - Today I am willing to be luckier than I've ever been before.
   - I commit to being luckier than I've ever been before.
   - Today, I am always in the right place at the right time for good luck to happen to me.

2. Write your commitment below: I, ________________, make a sincere commitment to being lucky, now and forever.

____

____

3. The action steps for my 30-day Goal that I am focusing on today are:

____

____

4. I will mix up my routine today by doing the following activities (if necessary, review your list at the beginning of Chapter 5):

____

____

5. The Bold Actions I will take today toward my Luck-Worthy Goal(s) are:

____

____

6. To attract greater luck to myself, I will start my day full of gratitude. Three things I am grateful for in my life are:

____

____

Luck Tracker: *EVENING*

1. Luck Inventory: Record synchronicities, breakthroughs, right place/right time events—anything that felt lucky. Or simply appreciate your willingness to be lucky.

____

____

2. How did I use my inner GPS today? Did I access my intuition, connect to my essence pace, or feel guided by my values? Write down any instances below:

____

____

3. How did I connect with my lucky community today? Check mark one or more.
   - Via interaction (virtual or otherwise) or by posting on a group FB page
   - By talking to or texting my accountability partner or mastermind group
   - By reading 5–10 pages of a book or listening to a podcast
   - ______________________________

4. Who can I/did I appreciate today, and how? (email, text, in person, mail, or phone)

____

5. Review your calendar for tomorrow and write the lucky outcomes you desire:

____

____

____

6. **Evening Luck Meditation:** To help your subconscious absorb luck-attracting concepts while you sleep, play the Evening Meditation recording or take three deep belly-breaths and say each of these phrases to yourself, silently or aloud, three times:
   - I AM lucky.
   - I deserve to be lucky.
   - I see lucky opportunities around me.
   - I trust my inner guidance.
   - I see luck in every situation.

Now drift off to a lucky slumber.

Day ______ **Date:** ____________

Luck Tracker: ***MORNING***

1. **Morning Luck Meditation**: To reinforce your willingness and commitment to being luckier, play the Conscious Luck Morning Activation Meditation recording or take three deep belly-breaths and say each of these phrases to yourself three times, silently or out loud:
   - Today I am willing to be luckier than I've ever been before.
   - I commit to being luckier than I've ever been before.
   - Today, I am always in the right place at the right time for good luck to happen to me.

2. Write your commitment below: I, ____________, make a sincere commitment to being lucky, now and forever.

____

____

3. The action steps for my 30-day Goal that I am focusing on today are:

____

____

4. I will mix up my routine today by doing the following activities (if necessary, review your list at the beginning of Chapter 5):

____

____

5. The Bold Actions I will take today toward my Luck-Worthy Goal(s) are:

____

____

6. To attract greater luck to myself, I will start my day full of gratitude. Three things I am grateful for in my life are:

____

____

Luck Tracker: *EVENING*

1. Luck Inventory: Record synchronicities, breakthroughs, right place/right time events—anything that felt lucky. Or simply appreciate your willingness to be lucky.

____

____

2. How did I use my inner GPS today? Did I access my intuition, connect to my essence pace, or feel guided by my values? Write down any instances below:

____

____

3. How did I connect with my lucky community today? Check mark one or more.
   - Via interaction (virtual or otherwise) or by posting on a group FB page
   - By talking to or texting my accountability partner or mastermind group
   - By reading 5–10 pages of a book or listening to a podcast
   - ____

4. Who can I/did I appreciate today, and how? (email, text, in person, mail, or phone)

____

5. Review your calendar for tomorrow and write the lucky outcomes you desire:

____

____

____

6. **Evening Luck Meditation:** To help your subconscious absorb luck-attracting concepts while you sleep, play the Evening Meditation recording or take three deep belly-breaths and say each of these phrases to yourself, silently or aloud, three times:
   - I AM lucky.
   - I deserve to be lucky.
   - I see lucky opportunities around me.
   - I trust my inner guidance.
   - I see luck in every situation.

Now drift off to a lucky slumber.

Day ________ **Date:** ________________

Luck Tracker: *MORNING*

1. **Morning Luck Meditation**: To reinforce your willingness and commitment to being luckier, play the Conscious Luck Morning Activation Meditation recording or take three deep belly-breaths and say each of these phrases to yourself three times, silently or out loud:
   - Today I am willing to be luckier than I've ever been before.
   - I commit to being luckier than I've ever been before.
   - Today, I am always in the right place at the right time for good luck to happen to me.

2. Write your commitment below: I, ________________, make a sincere commitment to being lucky, now and forever.

____

____

3. The action steps for my 30-day Goal that I am focusing on today are:

____

____

4. I will mix up my routine today by doing the following activities (if necessary, review your list at the beginning of Chapter 5):

____

____

5. The Bold Actions I will take today toward my Luck-Worthy Goal(s) are:

____

____

6. To attract greater luck to myself, I will start my day full of gratitude. Three things I am grateful for in my life are:

____

____

Luck Tracker: *EVENING*

1. Luck Inventory: Record synchronicities, breakthroughs, right place/right time events—anything that felt lucky. Or simply appreciate your willingness to be lucky.

____

____

2. How did I use my inner GPS today? Did I access my intuition, connect to my essence pace, or feel guided by my values? Write down any instances below:

____

____

3. How did I connect with my lucky community today? Check mark one or more.
   - Via interaction (virtual or otherwise) or by posting on a group FB page
   - By talking to or texting my accountability partner or mastermind group
   - By reading 5–10 pages of a book or listening to a podcast
   - ____

4. Who can I/did I appreciate today, and how? (email, text, in person, mail, or phone)

____

5. Review your calendar for tomorrow and write the lucky outcomes you desire:

____

____

____

6. **Evening Luck Meditation:** To help your subconscious absorb luck-attracting concepts while you sleep, play the Evening Meditation recording or take three deep belly-breaths and say each of these phrases to yourself, silently or aloud, three times:
   - I AM lucky.
   - I deserve to be lucky.
   - I see lucky opportunities around me.
   - I trust my inner guidance.
   - I see luck in every situation.

Now drift off to a lucky slumber.

Day ________ **Date:** __________________

Luck Tracker: ***MORNING***

1. **Morning Luck Meditation**: To reinforce your willingness and commitment to being luckier, play the Conscious Luck Morning Activation Meditation recording or take three deep belly-breaths and say each of these phrases to yourself three times, silently or out loud:
   - Today I am willing to be luckier than I've ever been before.
   - I commit to being luckier than I've ever been before.
   - Today, I am always in the right place at the right time for good luck to happen to me.

2. Write your commitment below: I, __________________, make a sincere commitment to being lucky, now and forever.

____

____

3. The action steps for my 30-day Goal that I am focusing on today are:

____

____

4. I will mix up my routine today by doing the following activities (if necessary, review your list at the beginning of Chapter 5):

____

____

5. The Bold Actions I will take today toward my Luck-Worthy Goal(s) are:

____

____

6. To attract greater luck to myself, I will start my day full of gratitude. Three things I am grateful for in my life are:

____

____

Luck Tracker: *EVENING*

1. Luck Inventory: Record synchronicities, breakthroughs, right place/right time events—anything that felt lucky. Or simply appreciate your willingness to be lucky.

____

____

2. How did I use my inner GPS today? Did I access my intuition, connect to my essence pace, or feel guided by my values? Write down any instances below:

____

____

3. How did I connect with my lucky community today? Check mark one or more.
   - Via interaction (virtual or otherwise) or by posting on a group FB page
   - By talking to or texting my accountability partner or mastermind group
   - By reading 5–10 pages of a book or listening to a podcast
   - ____

4. Who can I/did I appreciate today, and how? (email, text, in person, mail, or phone)

____

5. Review your calendar for tomorrow and write the lucky outcomes you desire:

____

____

____

6. **Evening Luck Meditation:** To help your subconscious absorb luck-attracting concepts while you sleep, play the Evening Meditation recording or take three deep belly-breaths and say each of these phrases to yourself, silently or aloud, three times:
   - I AM lucky.
   - I deserve to be lucky.
   - I see lucky opportunities around me.
   - I trust my inner guidance.
   - I see luck in every situation.

Now drift off to a lucky slumber.

Day ________ **Date:** __________________

Luck Tracker: ***MORNING***

1. **Morning Luck Meditation**: To reinforce your willingness and commitment to being luckier, play the Conscious Luck Morning Activation Meditation recording or take three deep belly-breaths and say each of these phrases to yourself three times, silently or out loud:
   - Today I am willing to be luckier than I've ever been before.
   - I commit to being luckier than I've ever been before.
   - Today, I am always in the right place at the right time for good luck to happen to me.

2. Write your commitment below: I, __________________, make a sincere commitment to being lucky, now and forever.

____

____

3. The action steps for my 30-day Goal that I am focusing on today are:

____

____

4. I will mix up my routine today by doing the following activities (if necessary, review your list at the beginning of Chapter 5):

____

____

5. The Bold Actions I will take today toward my Luck-Worthy Goal(s) are:

____

____

6. To attract greater luck to myself, I will start my day full of gratitude. Three things I am grateful for in my life are:

____

____

Luck Tracker: *EVENING*

1. Luck Inventory: Record synchronicities, breakthroughs, right place/right time events—anything that felt lucky. Or simply appreciate your willingness to be lucky.

 ____

 ____

2. How did I use my inner GPS today? Did I access my intuition, connect to my essence pace, or feel guided by my values? Write down any instances below:

 ____

 ____

3. How did I connect with my lucky community today? Check mark one or more.
    - Via interaction (virtual or otherwise) or by posting on a group FB page
    - By talking to or texting my accountability partner or mastermind group
    - By reading 5–10 pages of a book or listening to a podcast
    - ____

4. Who can I/did I appreciate today, and how? (email, text, in person, mail, or phone)

 ____

5. Review your calendar for tomorrow and write the lucky outcomes you desire:

 ____

 ____

 ____

6. **Evening Luck Meditation:** To help your subconscious absorb luck-attracting concepts while you sleep, play the Evening Meditation recording or take three deep belly-breaths and say each of these phrases to yourself, silently or aloud, three times:
    - I AM lucky.
    - I deserve to be lucky.
    - I see lucky opportunities around me.
    - I trust my inner guidance.
    - I see luck in every situation.

Now drift off to a lucky slumber.

Day ________ **Date:** ________________

Luck Tracker: ***MORNING***

1. **Morning Luck Meditation**: To reinforce your willingness and commitment to being luckier, play the Conscious Luck Morning Activation Meditation recording or take three deep belly-breaths and say each of these phrases to yourself three times, silently or out loud:
   - Today I am willing to be luckier than I've ever been before.
   - I commit to being luckier than I've ever been before.
   - Today, I am always in the right place at the right time for good luck to happen to me.

2. Write your commitment below: I, ________________, make a sincere commitment to being lucky, now and forever.

____

____

3. The action steps for my 30-day Goal that I am focusing on today are:

____

____

4. I will mix up my routine today by doing the following activities (if necessary, review your list at the beginning of Chapter 5):

____

____

5. The Bold Actions I will take today toward my Luck-Worthy Goal(s) are:

____

____

6. To attract greater luck to myself, I will start my day full of gratitude. Three things I am grateful for in my life are:

____

____

Luck Tracker: *EVENING*

1. Luck Inventory: Record synchronicities, breakthroughs, right place/right time events—anything that felt lucky. Or simply appreciate your willingness to be lucky.

____

____

2. How did I use my inner GPS today? Did I access my intuition, connect to my essence pace, or feel guided by my values? Write down any instances below:

____

____

3. How did I connect with my lucky community today? Check mark one or more.
    - Via interaction (virtual or otherwise) or by posting on a group FB page
    - By talking to or texting my accountability partner or mastermind group
    - By reading 5–10 pages of a book or listening to a podcast
    - ____

4. Who can I/did I appreciate today, and how? (email, text, in person, mail, or phone)

____

5. Review your calendar for tomorrow and write the lucky outcomes you desire:

____

____

____

6. **Evening Luck Meditation:** To help your subconscious absorb luck-attracting concepts while you sleep, play the Evening Meditation recording or take three deep belly-breaths and say each of these phrases to yourself, silently or aloud, three times:
    - I AM lucky.
    - I deserve to be lucky.
    - I see lucky opportunities around me.
    - I trust my inner guidance.
    - I see luck in every situation.

Now drift off to a lucky slumber.

Day ________ **Date:** ________________

Luck Tracker: ***MORNING***

1. **Morning Luck Meditation**: To reinforce your willingness and commitment to being luckier, play the Conscious Luck Morning Activation Meditation recording or take three deep belly-breaths and say each of these phrases to yourself three times, silently or out loud:
    - Today I am willing to be luckier than I've ever been before.
    - I commit to being luckier than I've ever been before.
    - Today, I am always in the right place at the right time for good luck to happen to me.

2. Write your commitment below: I, ________________, make a sincere commitment to being lucky, now and forever.

____

____

3. The action steps for my 30-day Goal that I am focusing on today are:

____

____

4. I will mix up my routine today by doing the following activities (if necessary, review your list at the beginning of Chapter 5):

____

____

5. The Bold Actions I will take today toward my Luck-Worthy Goal(s) are:

____

____

6. To attract greater luck to myself, I will start my day full of gratitude. Three things I am grateful for in my life are:

____

____

Luck Tracker: ***EVENING***

1. Luck Inventory: Record synchronicities, breakthroughs, right place/right time events—anything that felt lucky. Or simply appreciate your willingness to be lucky.

___

___

2. How did I use my inner GPS today? Did I access my intuition, connect to my essence pace, or feel guided by my values? Write down any instances below:

___

___

3. How did I connect with my lucky community today? Check mark one or more.
    - Via interaction (virtual or otherwise) or by posting on a group FB page
    - By talking to or texting my accountability partner or mastermind group
    - By reading 5–10 pages of a book or listening to a podcast
    - ___

4. Who can I/did I appreciate today, and how? (email, text, in person, mail, or phone)

___

5. Review your calendar for tomorrow and write the lucky outcomes you desire:

___

___

___

6. **Evening Luck Meditation:** To help your subconscious absorb luck-attracting concepts while you sleep, play the Evening Meditation recording or take three deep belly-breaths and say each of these phrases to yourself, silently or aloud, three times:
    - I AM lucky.
    - I deserve to be lucky.
    - I see lucky opportunities around me.
    - I trust my inner guidance.
    - I see luck in every situation.

Now drift off to a lucky slumber.

Day ________ **Date:** ________________

Luck Tracker: ***MORNING***

1. **Morning Luck Meditation**: To reinforce your willingness and commitment to being luckier, play the Conscious Luck Morning Activation Meditation recording or take three deep belly-breaths and say each of these phrases to yourself three times, silently or out loud:
   - Today I am willing to be luckier than I've ever been before.
   - I commit to being luckier than I've ever been before.
   - Today, I am always in the right place at the right time for good luck to happen to me.

2. Write your commitment below: I, ________________, make a sincere commitment to being lucky, now and forever.

   ____

   ____

3. The action steps for my 30-day Goal that I am focusing on today are:

   ____

   ____

4. I will mix up my routine today by doing the following activities (if necessary, review your list at the beginning of Chapter 5):

   ____

   ____

5. The Bold Actions I will take today toward my Luck-Worthy Goal(s) are:

   ____

   ____

6. To attract greater luck to myself, I will start my day full of gratitude. Three things I am grateful for in my life are:

   ____

   ____

Luck Tracker: ***EVENING***

1. Luck Inventory: Record synchronicities, breakthroughs, right place/right time events—anything that felt lucky. Or simply appreciate your willingness to be lucky.

___

___

2. How did I use my inner GPS today? Did I access my intuition, connect to my essence pace, or feel guided by my values? Write down any instances below:

___

___

3. How did I connect with my lucky community today? Check mark one or more.
   - Via interaction (virtual or otherwise) or by posting on a group FB page
   - By talking to or texting my accountability partner or mastermind group
   - By reading 5–10 pages of a book or listening to a podcast
   - ___

4. Who can I/did I appreciate today, and how? (email, text, in person, mail, or phone)

___

5. Review your calendar for tomorrow and write the lucky outcomes you desire:

___

___

___

6. **Evening Luck Meditation:** To help your subconscious absorb luck-attracting concepts while you sleep, play the Evening Meditation recording or take three deep belly-breaths and say each of these phrases to yourself, silently or aloud, three times:
   - I AM lucky.
   - I deserve to be lucky.
   - I see lucky opportunities around me.
   - I trust my inner guidance.
   - I see luck in every situation.

Now drift off to a lucky slumber.

Day ________ **Date:** ________________

Luck Tracker: ***MORNING***

1. **Morning Luck Meditation**: To reinforce your willingness and commitment to being luckier, play the Conscious Luck Morning Activation Meditation recording or take three deep belly-breaths and say each of these phrases to yourself three times, silently or out loud:
   - Today I am willing to be luckier than I've ever been before.
   - I commit to being luckier than I've ever been before.
   - Today, I am always in the right place at the right time for good luck to happen to me.

2. Write your commitment below: I, ________________, make a sincere commitment to being lucky, now and forever.

____

____

3. The action steps for my 30-day Goal that I am focusing on today are:

____

____

4. I will mix up my routine today by doing the following activities (if necessary, review your list at the beginning of Chapter 5):

____

____

5. The Bold Actions I will take today toward my Luck-Worthy Goal(s) are:

____

____

6. To attract greater luck to myself, I will start my day full of gratitude. Three things I am grateful for in my life are:

____

____

Luck Tracker: *EVENING*

1. Luck Inventory: Record synchronicities, breakthroughs, right place/right time events—anything that felt lucky. Or simply appreciate your willingness to be lucky.

____

____

2. How did I use my inner GPS today? Did I access my intuition, connect to my essence pace, or feel guided by my values? Write down any instances below:

____

____

3. How did I connect with my lucky community today? Check mark one or more.
   - Via interaction (virtual or otherwise) or by posting on a group FB page
   - By talking to or texting my accountability partner or mastermind group
   - By reading 5–10 pages of a book or listening to a podcast
   - ______________________________

4. Who can I/did I appreciate today, and how? (email, text, in person, mail, or phone)

____

5. Review your calendar for tomorrow and write the lucky outcomes you desire:

____

____

____

6. **Evening Luck Meditation:** To help your subconscious absorb luck-attracting concepts while you sleep, play the Evening Meditation recording or take three deep belly-breaths and say each of these phrases to yourself, silently or aloud, three times:
   - I AM lucky.
   - I deserve to be lucky.
   - I see lucky opportunities around me.
   - I trust my inner guidance.
   - I see luck in every situation.

Now drift off to a lucky slumber.

Day ________ **Date:** ________________

Luck Tracker: ***MORNING***

1. **Morning Luck Meditation**: To reinforce your willingness and commitment to being luckier, play the Conscious Luck Morning Activation Meditation recording or take three deep belly-breaths and say each of these phrases to yourself three times, silently or out loud:
   - Today I am willing to be luckier than I've ever been before.
   - I commit to being luckier than I've ever been before.
   - Today, I am always in the right place at the right time for good luck to happen to me.
2. Write your commitment below: I, ________________, make a sincere commitment to being lucky, now and forever.

____

____

3. The action steps for my 30-day Goal that I am focusing on today are:

____

____

4. I will mix up my routine today by doing the following activities (if necessary, review your list at the beginning of Chapter 5):

____

____

5. The Bold Actions I will take today toward my Luck-Worthy Goal(s) are:

____

____

6. To attract greater luck to myself, I will start my day full of gratitude. Three things I am grateful for in my life are:

____

____

Luck Tracker: *EVENING*

1. Luck Inventory: Record synchronicities, breakthroughs, right place/right time events—anything that felt lucky. Or simply appreciate your willingness to be lucky.

____

____

2. How did I use my inner GPS today? Did I access my intuition, connect to my essence pace, or feel guided by my values? Write down any instances below:

____

____

3. How did I connect with my lucky community today? Check mark one or more.
   - Via interaction (virtual or otherwise) or by posting on a group FB page
   - By talking to or texting my accountability partner or mastermind group
   - By reading 5–10 pages of a book or listening to a podcast
   - ____________________

4. Who can I/did I appreciate today, and how? (email, text, in person, mail, or phone)

____

5. Review your calendar for tomorrow and write the lucky outcomes you desire:

____

____

____

6. **Evening Luck Meditation:** To help your subconscious absorb luck-attracting concepts while you sleep, play the Evening Meditation recording or take three deep belly-breaths and say each of these phrases to yourself, silently or aloud, three times:
   - I AM lucky.
   - I deserve to be lucky.
   - I see lucky opportunities around me.
   - I trust my inner guidance.
   - I see luck in every situation.

Now drift off to a lucky slumber.

Day ________ **Date:** __________________

Luck Tracker: ***MORNING***

1. **Morning Luck Meditation**: To reinforce your willingness and commitment to being luckier, play the Conscious Luck Morning Activation Meditation recording or take three deep belly-breaths and say each of these phrases to yourself three times, silently or out loud:
   - Today I am willing to be luckier than I've ever been before.
   - I commit to being luckier than I've ever been before.
   - Today, I am always in the right place at the right time for good luck to happen to me.

2. Write your commitment below: I, ________________, make a sincere commitment to being lucky, now and forever.

____

____

3. The action steps for my 30-day Goal that I am focusing on today are:

____

____

4. I will mix up my routine today by doing the following activities (if necessary, review your list at the beginning of Chapter 5):

____

____

5. The Bold Actions I will take today toward my Luck-Worthy Goal(s) are:

____

____

6. To attract greater luck to myself, I will start my day full of gratitude. Three things I am grateful for in my life are:

____

____

Luck Tracker: *EVENING*

1. Luck Inventory: Record synchronicities, breakthroughs, right place/right time events—anything that felt lucky. Or simply appreciate your willingness to be lucky.

____

____

2. How did I use my inner GPS today? Did I access my intuition, connect to my essence pace, or feel guided by my values? Write down any instances below:

____

____

3. How did I connect with my lucky community today? Check mark one or more.
   - Via interaction (virtual or otherwise) or by posting on a group FB page
   - By talking to or texting my accountability partner or mastermind group
   - By reading 5–10 pages of a book or listening to a podcast
   - ____

4. Who can I/did I appreciate today, and how? (email, text, in person, mail, or phone)

____

5. Review your calendar for tomorrow and write the lucky outcomes you desire:

____

____

____

6. **Evening Luck Meditation:** To help your subconscious absorb luck-attracting concepts while you sleep, play the Evening Meditation recording or take three deep belly-breaths and say each of these phrases to yourself, silently or aloud, three times:
   - I AM lucky.
   - I deserve to be lucky.
   - I see lucky opportunities around me.
   - I trust my inner guidance.
   - I see luck in every situation.

Now drift off to a lucky slumber.

Day ________ **Date:** ________________

Luck Tracker: ***MORNING***

1. **Morning Luck Meditation**: To reinforce your willingness and commitment to being luckier, play the Conscious Luck Morning Activation Meditation recording or take three deep belly-breaths and say each of these phrases to yourself three times, silently or out loud:
   - Today I am willing to be luckier than I've ever been before.
   - I commit to being luckier than I've ever been before.
   - Today, I am always in the right place at the right time for good luck to happen to me.

2. Write your commitment below: I, ________________, make a sincere commitment to being lucky, now and forever.

____

____

3. The action steps for my 30-day Goal that I am focusing on today are:

____

____

4. I will mix up my routine today by doing the following activities (if necessary, review your list at the beginning of Chapter 5):

____

____

5. The Bold Actions I will take today toward my Luck-Worthy Goal(s) are:

____

____

6. To attract greater luck to myself, I will start my day full of gratitude. Three things I am grateful for in my life are:

____

____

Luck Tracker: *EVENING*

1. Luck Inventory: Record synchronicities, breakthroughs, right place/right time events—anything that felt lucky. Or simply appreciate your willingness to be lucky.

____

____

2. How did I use my inner GPS today? Did I access my intuition, connect to my essence pace, or feel guided by my values? Write down any instances below:

____

____

3. How did I connect with my lucky community today? Check mark one or more.
   - Via interaction (virtual or otherwise) or by posting on a group FB page
   - By talking to or texting my accountability partner or mastermind group
   - By reading 5–10 pages of a book or listening to a podcast
   - ____________________________________

4. Who can I/did I appreciate today, and how? (email, text, in person, mail, or phone)

____

5. Review your calendar for tomorrow and write the lucky outcomes you desire:

____

____

____

6. **Evening Luck Meditation:** To help your subconscious absorb luck-attracting concepts while you sleep, play the Evening Meditation recording or take three deep belly-breaths and say each of these phrases to yourself, silently or aloud, three times:
   - I AM lucky.
   - I deserve to be lucky.
   - I see lucky opportunities around me.
   - I trust my inner guidance.
   - I see luck in every situation.

Now drift off to a lucky slumber.

Day ________ **Date:** ________________

Luck Tracker: ***MORNING***

1. **Morning Luck Meditation**: To reinforce your willingness and commitment to being luckier, play the Conscious Luck Morning Activation Meditation recording or take three deep belly-breaths and say each of these phrases to yourself three times, silently or out loud:
   - Today I am willing to be luckier than I've ever been before.
   - I commit to being luckier than I've ever been before.
   - Today, I am always in the right place at the right time for good luck to happen to me.

2. Write your commitment below: I, ________________, make a sincere commitment to being lucky, now and forever.

   ____

   ____

3. The action steps for my 30-day Goal that I am focusing on today are:

   ____

   ____

4. I will mix up my routine today by doing the following activities (if necessary, review your list at the beginning of Chapter 5):

   ____

   ____

5. The Bold Actions I will take today toward my Luck-Worthy Goal(s) are:

   ____

   ____

6. To attract greater luck to myself, I will start my day full of gratitude. Three things I am grateful for in my life are:

   ____

   ____

Luck Tracker: *EVENING*

1. Luck Inventory: Record synchronicities, breakthroughs, right place/right time events—anything that felt lucky. Or simply appreciate your willingness to be lucky.

____

____

2. How did I use my inner GPS today? Did I access my intuition, connect to my essence pace, or feel guided by my values? Write down any instances below:

____

____

3. How did I connect with my lucky community today? Check mark one or more.
   - Via interaction (virtual or otherwise) or by posting on a group FB page
   - By talking to or texting my accountability partner or mastermind group
   - By reading 5–10 pages of a book or listening to a podcast
   - ____________________________________

4. Who can I/did I appreciate today, and how? (email, text, in person, mail, or phone)

____

5. Review your calendar for tomorrow and write the lucky outcomes you desire:

____

____

____

6. **Evening Luck Meditation:** To help your subconscious absorb luck-attracting concepts while you sleep, play the Evening Meditation recording or take three deep belly-breaths and say each of these phrases to yourself, silently or aloud, three times:
   - I AM lucky.
   - I deserve to be lucky.
   - I see lucky opportunities around me.
   - I trust my inner guidance.
   - I see luck in every situation.

Now drift off to a lucky slumber.

Day ________ **Date:** ________________

Luck Tracker: ***MORNING***

1. **Morning Luck Meditation**: To reinforce your willingness and commitment to being luckier, play the Conscious Luck Morning Activation Meditation recording or take three deep belly-breaths and say each of these phrases to yourself three times, silently or out loud:
   - Today I am willing to be luckier than I've ever been before.
   - I commit to being luckier than I've ever been before.
   - Today, I am always in the right place at the right time for good luck to happen to me.

2. Write your commitment below: I, ________________, make a sincere commitment to being lucky, now and forever.

____

____

3. The action steps for my 30-day Goal that I am focusing on today are:

____

____

4. I will mix up my routine today by doing the following activities (if necessary, review your list at the beginning of Chapter 5):

____

____

5. The Bold Actions I will take today toward my Luck-Worthy Goal(s) are:

____

____

6. To attract greater luck to myself, I will start my day full of gratitude. Three things I am grateful for in my life are:

____

____

Luck Tracker: *EVENING*

1. Luck Inventory: Record synchronicities, breakthroughs, right place/right time events—anything that felt lucky. Or simply appreciate your willingness to be lucky.

____

____

2. How did I use my inner GPS today? Did I access my intuition, connect to my essence pace, or feel guided by my values? Write down any instances below:

____

____

3. How did I connect with my lucky community today? Check mark one or more.
   - Via interaction (virtual or otherwise) or by posting on a group FB page
   - By talking to or texting my accountability partner or mastermind group
   - By reading 5–10 pages of a book or listening to a podcast
   - ____

4. Who can I/did I appreciate today, and how? (email, text, in person, mail, or phone)

____

5. Review your calendar for tomorrow and write the lucky outcomes you desire:

____

____

____

6. **Evening Luck Meditation:** To help your subconscious absorb luck-attracting concepts while you sleep, play the Evening Meditation recording or take three deep belly-breaths and say each of these phrases to yourself, silently or aloud, three times:
   - I AM lucky.
   - I deserve to be lucky.
   - I see lucky opportunities around me.
   - I trust my inner guidance.
   - I see luck in every situation.

Now drift off to a lucky slumber.

Day ________ **Date:** ________________

Luck Tracker: ***MORNING***

1. **Morning Luck Meditation**: To reinforce your willingness and commitment to being luckier, play the Conscious Luck Morning Activation Meditation recording or take three deep belly-breaths and say each of these phrases to yourself three times, silently or out loud:
   - Today I am willing to be luckier than I've ever been before.
   - I commit to being luckier than I've ever been before.
   - Today, I am always in the right place at the right time for good luck to happen to me.

2. Write your commitment below: I, ________________, make a sincere commitment to being lucky, now and forever.

   ____

   ____

3. The action steps for my 30-day Goal that I am focusing on today are:

   ____

   ____

4. I will mix up my routine today by doing the following activities (if necessary, review your list at the beginning of Chapter 5):

   ____

   ____

5. The Bold Actions I will take today toward my Luck-Worthy Goal(s) are:

   ____

   ____

6. To attract greater luck to myself, I will start my day full of gratitude. Three things I am grateful for in my life are:

   ____

   ____

Luck Tracker: *EVENING*

1. Luck Inventory: Record synchronicities, breakthroughs, right place/right time events—anything that felt lucky. Or simply appreciate your willingness to be lucky.

____

____

2. How did I use my inner GPS today? Did I access my intuition, connect to my essence pace, or feel guided by my values? Write down any instances below:

____

____

3. How did I connect with my lucky community today? Check mark one or more.
   - Via interaction (virtual or otherwise) or by posting on a group FB page
   - By talking to or texting my accountability partner or mastermind group
   - By reading 5–10 pages of a book or listening to a podcast
   - ______________________________

4. Who can I/did I appreciate today, and how? (email, text, in person, mail, or phone)

____

5. Review your calendar for tomorrow and write the lucky outcomes you desire:

____

____

____

6. **Evening Luck Meditation:** To help your subconscious absorb luck-attracting concepts while you sleep, play the Evening Meditation recording or take three deep belly-breaths and say each of these phrases to yourself, silently or aloud, three times:
   - I AM lucky.
   - I deserve to be lucky.
   - I see lucky opportunities around me.
   - I trust my inner guidance.
   - I see luck in every situation.

Now drift off to a lucky slumber.

Day ________ **Date:** ________________

Luck Tracker: ***MORNING***

1. **Morning Luck Meditation**: To reinforce your willingness and commitment to being luckier, play the Conscious Luck Morning Activation Meditation recording or take three deep belly-breaths and say each of these phrases to yourself three times, silently or out loud:
   - Today I am willing to be luckier than I've ever been before.
   - I commit to being luckier than I've ever been before.
   - Today, I am always in the right place at the right time for good luck to happen to me.

2. Write your commitment below: I, ________________, make a sincere commitment to being lucky, now and forever.

   ____

   ____

3. The action steps for my 30-day Goal that I am focusing on today are:

   ____

   ____

4. I will mix up my routine today by doing the following activities (if necessary, review your list at the beginning of Chapter 5):

   ____

   ____

5. The Bold Actions I will take today toward my Luck-Worthy Goal(s) are:

   ____

   ____

6. To attract greater luck to myself, I will start my day full of gratitude. Three things I am grateful for in my life are:

   ____

   ____

Luck Tracker: *EVENING*

1. Luck Inventory: Record synchronicities, breakthroughs, right place/right time events—anything that felt lucky. Or simply appreciate your willingness to be lucky.

____

____

2. How did I use my inner GPS today? Did I access my intuition, connect to my essence pace, or feel guided by my values? Write down any instances below:

____

____

3. How did I connect with my lucky community today? Check mark one or more.
   - Via interaction (virtual or otherwise) or by posting on a group FB page
   - By talking to or texting my accountability partner or mastermind group
   - By reading 5–10 pages of a book or listening to a podcast
   - ____

4. Who can I/did I appreciate today, and how? (email, text, in person, mail, or phone)

____

5. Review your calendar for tomorrow and write the lucky outcomes you desire:

____

____

____

6. **Evening Luck Meditation:** To help your subconscious absorb luck-attracting concepts while you sleep, play the Evening Meditation recording or take three deep belly-breaths and say each of these phrases to yourself, silently or aloud, three times:
   - I AM lucky.
   - I deserve to be lucky.
   - I see lucky opportunities around me.
   - I trust my inner guidance.
   - I see luck in every situation.

Now drift off to a lucky slumber.

Day ________ **Date:** __________________

Luck Tracker: ***MORNING***

1. **Morning Luck Meditation**: To reinforce your willingness and commitment to being luckier, play the Conscious Luck Morning Activation Meditation recording or take three deep belly-breaths and say each of these phrases to yourself three times, silently or out loud:
   - Today I am willing to be luckier than I've ever been before.
   - I commit to being luckier than I've ever been before.
   - Today, I am always in the right place at the right time for good luck to happen to me.

2. Write your commitment below: I, __________________, make a sincere commitment to being lucky, now and forever.

____

____

3. The action steps for my 30-day Goal that I am focusing on today are:

____

____

4. I will mix up my routine today by doing the following activities (if necessary, review your list at the beginning of Chapter 5):

____

____

5. The Bold Actions I will take today toward my Luck-Worthy Goal(s) are:

____

____

6. To attract greater luck to myself, I will start my day full of gratitude. Three things I am grateful for in my life are:

____

____

Luck Tracker: *EVENING*

1. Luck Inventory: Record synchronicities, breakthroughs, right place/right time events—anything that felt lucky. Or simply appreciate your willingness to be lucky.

____

____

2. How did I use my inner GPS today? Did I access my intuition, connect to my essence pace, or feel guided by my values? Write down any instances below:

____

____

3. How did I connect with my lucky community today? Check mark one or more.
   - Via interaction (virtual or otherwise) or by posting on a group FB page
   - By talking to or texting my accountability partner or mastermind group
   - By reading 5–10 pages of a book or listening to a podcast
   - ____

4. Who can I/did I appreciate today, and how? (email, text, in person, mail, or phone)

____

5. Review your calendar for tomorrow and write the lucky outcomes you desire:

____

____

____

6. **Evening Luck Meditation:** To help your subconscious absorb luck-attracting concepts while you sleep, play the Evening Meditation recording or take three deep belly-breaths and say each of these phrases to yourself, silently or aloud, three times:
   - I AM lucky.
   - I deserve to be lucky.
   - I see lucky opportunities around me.
   - I trust my inner guidance.
   - I see luck in every situation.

Now drift off to a lucky slumber.

Day ________ **Date:** ________________

Luck Tracker: ***MORNING***

1. **Morning Luck Meditation**: To reinforce your willingness and commitment to being luckier, play the Conscious Luck Morning Activation Meditation recording or take three deep belly-breaths and say each of these phrases to yourself three times, silently or out loud:
   - Today I am willing to be luckier than I've ever been before.
   - I commit to being luckier than I've ever been before.
   - Today, I am always in the right place at the right time for good luck to happen to me.

2. Write your commitment below: I, ________________, make a sincere commitment to being lucky, now and forever.

____

____

3. The action steps for my 30-day Goal that I am focusing on today are:

____

____

4. I will mix up my routine today by doing the following activities (if necessary, review your list at the beginning of Chapter 5):

____

____

5. The Bold Actions I will take today toward my Luck-Worthy Goal(s) are:

____

____

6. To attract greater luck to myself, I will start my day full of gratitude. Three things I am grateful for in my life are:

____

____

Luck Tracker: *EVENING*

1. Luck Inventory: Record synchronicities, breakthroughs, right place/right time events—anything that felt lucky. Or simply appreciate your willingness to be lucky.

____

____

2. How did I use my inner GPS today? Did I access my intuition, connect to my essence pace, or feel guided by my values? Write down any instances below:

____

____

3. How did I connect with my lucky community today? Check mark one or more.
   - Via interaction (virtual or otherwise) or by posting on a group FB page
   - By talking to or texting my accountability partner or mastermind group
   - By reading 5–10 pages of a book or listening to a podcast
   - ____

4. Who can I/did I appreciate today, and how? (email, text, in person, mail, or phone)

____

5. Review your calendar for tomorrow and write the lucky outcomes you desire:

____

____

____

6. **Evening Luck Meditation:** To help your subconscious absorb luck-attracting concepts while you sleep, play the Evening Meditation recording or take three deep belly-breaths and say each of these phrases to yourself, silently or aloud, three times:
   - I AM lucky.
   - I deserve to be lucky.
   - I see lucky opportunities around me.
   - I trust my inner guidance.
   - I see luck in every situation.

Now drift off to a lucky slumber.

Day ________ **Date:** ________________

Luck Tracker: ***MORNING***

1. **Morning Luck Meditation**: To reinforce your willingness and commitment to being luckier, play the Conscious Luck Morning Activation Meditation recording or take three deep belly-breaths and say each of these phrases to yourself three times, silently or out loud:
   - Today I am willing to be luckier than I've ever been before.
   - I commit to being luckier than I've ever been before.
   - Today, I am always in the right place at the right time for good luck to happen to me.

2. Write your commitment below: I, ________________, make a sincere commitment to being lucky, now and forever.

____

____

3. The action steps for my 30-day Goal that I am focusing on today are:

____

____

4. I will mix up my routine today by doing the following activities (if necessary, review your list at the beginning of Chapter 5):

____

____

5. The Bold Actions I will take today toward my Luck-Worthy Goal(s) are:

____

____

6. To attract greater luck to myself, I will start my day full of gratitude. Three things I am grateful for in my life are:

____

____

Luck Tracker: ***EVENING***

1. Luck Inventory: Record synchronicities, breakthroughs, right place/right time events—anything that felt lucky. Or simply appreciate your willingness to be lucky.

____

____

2. How did I use my inner GPS today? Did I access my intuition, connect to my essence pace, or feel guided by my values? Write down any instances below:

____

____

3. How did I connect with my lucky community today? Check mark one or more.
   - Via interaction (virtual or otherwise) or by posting on a group FB page
   - By talking to or texting my accountability partner or mastermind group
   - By reading 5–10 pages of a book or listening to a podcast
   - ____

4. Who can I/did I appreciate today, and how? (email, text, in person, mail, or phone)

____

5. Review your calendar for tomorrow and write the lucky outcomes you desire:

____

____

____

6. **Evening Luck Meditation:** To help your subconscious absorb luck-attracting concepts while you sleep, play the Evening Meditation recording or take three deep belly-breaths and say each of these phrases to yourself, silently or aloud, three times:
   - I AM lucky.
   - I deserve to be lucky.
   - I see lucky opportunities around me.
   - I trust my inner guidance.
   - I see luck in every situation.

Now drift off to a lucky slumber.

Day ________ **Date:** ________________

Luck Tracker: ***MORNING***

1. **Morning Luck Meditation**: To reinforce your willingness and commitment to being luckier, play the Conscious Luck Morning Activation Meditation recording or take three deep belly-breaths and say each of these phrases to yourself three times, silently or out loud:
   - Today I am willing to be luckier than I've ever been before.
   - I commit to being luckier than I've ever been before.
   - Today, I am always in the right place at the right time for good luck to happen to me.
2. Write your commitment below: I, ________________, make a sincere commitment to being lucky, now and forever.

____

____

3. The action steps for my 30-day Goal that I am focusing on today are:

____

____

4. I will mix up my routine today by doing the following activities (if necessary, review your list at the beginning of Chapter 5):

____

____

5. The Bold Actions I will take today toward my Luck-Worthy Goal(s) are:

____

____

6. To attract greater luck to myself, I will start my day full of gratitude. Three things I am grateful for in my life are:

____

____

Luck Tracker: *EVENING*

1. Luck Inventory: Record synchronicities, breakthroughs, right place/right time events—anything that felt lucky. Or simply appreciate your willingness to be lucky.

____

____

2. How did I use my inner GPS today? Did I access my intuition, connect to my essence pace, or feel guided by my values? Write down any instances below:

____

____

3. How did I connect with my lucky community today? Check mark one or more.
    - Via interaction (virtual or otherwise) or by posting on a group FB page
    - By talking to or texting my accountability partner or mastermind group
    - By reading 5–10 pages of a book or listening to a podcast
    - ______________________________

4. Who can I/did I appreciate today, and how? (email, text, in person, mail, or phone)

____

5. Review your calendar for tomorrow and write the lucky outcomes you desire:

____

____

____

6. **Evening Luck Meditation:** To help your subconscious absorb luck-attracting concepts while you sleep, play the Evening Meditation recording or take three deep belly-breaths and say each of these phrases to yourself, silently or aloud, three times:
    - I AM lucky.
    - I deserve to be lucky.
    - I see lucky opportunities around me.
    - I trust my inner guidance.
    - I see luck in every situation.

Now drift off to a lucky slumber.

Day ________ **Date:** ________________

Luck Tracker: ***MORNING***

1. **Morning Luck Meditation**: To reinforce your willingness and commitment to being luckier, play the Conscious Luck Morning Activation Meditation recording or take three deep belly-breaths and say each of these phrases to yourself three times, silently or out loud:
   - Today I am willing to be luckier than I've ever been before.
   - I commit to being luckier than I've ever been before.
   - Today, I am always in the right place at the right time for good luck to happen to me.

2. Write your commitment below: I, ________________, make a sincere commitment to being lucky, now and forever.

____

____

3. The action steps for my 30-day Goal that I am focusing on today are:

____

____

4. I will mix up my routine today by doing the following activities (if necessary, review your list at the beginning of Chapter 5):

____

____

5. The Bold Actions I will take today toward my Luck-Worthy Goal(s) are:

____

____

6. To attract greater luck to myself, I will start my day full of gratitude. Three things I am grateful for in my life are:

____

____

Luck Tracker: *EVENING*

1. Luck Inventory: Record synchronicities, breakthroughs, right place/right time events—anything that felt lucky. Or simply appreciate your willingness to be lucky.

____

____

2. How did I use my inner GPS today? Did I access my intuition, connect to my essence pace, or feel guided by my values? Write down any instances below:

____

____

3. How did I connect with my lucky community today? Check mark one or more.
   - Via interaction (virtual or otherwise) or by posting on a group FB page
   - By talking to or texting my accountability partner or mastermind group
   - By reading 5–10 pages of a book or listening to a podcast
   - ______________________________

4. Who can I/did I appreciate today, and how? (email, text, in person, mail, or phone)

____

5. Review your calendar for tomorrow and write the lucky outcomes you desire:

____

____

____

6. **Evening Luck Meditation:** To help your subconscious absorb luck-attracting concepts while you sleep, play the Evening Meditation recording or take three deep belly-breaths and say each of these phrases to yourself, silently or aloud, three times:
   - I AM lucky.
   - I deserve to be lucky.
   - I see lucky opportunities around me.
   - I trust my inner guidance.
   - I see luck in every situation.

Now drift off to a lucky slumber.

Day ________ **Date:** ________________

Luck Tracker: ***MORNING***

1. **Morning Luck Meditation**: To reinforce your willingness and commitment to being luckier, play the Conscious Luck Morning Activation Meditation recording or take three deep belly-breaths and say each of these phrases to yourself three times, silently or out loud:
   - Today I am willing to be luckier than I've ever been before.
   - I commit to being luckier than I've ever been before.
   - Today, I am always in the right place at the right time for good luck to happen to me.
2. Write your commitment below: I, ________________, make a sincere commitment to being lucky, now and forever.

   ____

   ____

3. The action steps for my 30-day Goal that I am focusing on today are:

   ____

   ____

4. I will mix up my routine today by doing the following activities (if necessary, review your list at the beginning of Chapter 5):

   ____

   ____

5. The Bold Actions I will take today toward my Luck-Worthy Goal(s) are:

   ____

   ____

6. To attract greater luck to myself, I will start my day full of gratitude. Three things I am grateful for in my life are:

   ____

   ____

Luck Tracker: *EVENING*

1. Luck Inventory: Record synchronicities, breakthroughs, right place/right time events—anything that felt lucky. Or simply appreciate your willingness to be lucky.

___

___

2. How did I use my inner GPS today? Did I access my intuition, connect to my essence pace, or feel guided by my values? Write down any instances below:

___

___

3. How did I connect with my lucky community today? Check mark one or more.
   - Via interaction (virtual or otherwise) or by posting on a group FB page
   - By talking to or texting my accountability partner or mastermind group
   - By reading 5–10 pages of a book or listening to a podcast
   - ___

4. Who can I/did I appreciate today, and how? (email, text, in person, mail, or phone)

___

5. Review your calendar for tomorrow and write the lucky outcomes you desire:

___

___

___

6. **Evening Luck Meditation:** To help your subconscious absorb luck-attracting concepts while you sleep, play the Evening Meditation recording or take three deep belly-breaths and say each of these phrases to yourself, silently or aloud, three times:
   - I AM lucky.
   - I deserve to be lucky.
   - I see lucky opportunities around me.
   - I trust my inner guidance.
   - I see luck in every situation.

Now drift off to a lucky slumber.

CONSCIOUS LUCK RESOURCES

Website Resources, Meditation Links, and More

Here are additional materials and information to further support you on your Conscious Luck journey. The following pages can also be used as a quick reference guide for all the links provided throughout the workbook.

Workbook Web Page

We've created a dedicated website for the materials mentioned in this workbook. To access it, go to www.consciousluck.com/workbook, where you'll be asked for your name and email address. Once we receive those, we'll send you the URL where you can find all of the additional content we've created for you, so please make sure to provide a valid email address. Please bookmark the page so you can return easily (and frequently) to make use of the resources there.

Here are some of the resources on the site:

- ***The Conscious Luck Shame-Transforming Process***: We've provided different recordings of the same meditation, in the authors' voices. Feel free to listen to any of the recordings. You may want to switch between them, depending on whose voice you resonate with most at the time you plan to listen.
- ***The Conscious Luck Heart Meditation***: Do this meditation whenever you are creating new luck-worthy goals to determine if your goal lights

you up, fulfilling Luck-Worthy Goal Requirement #2. Again, you can choose between different recordings of the same meditation, done in the authors' voices.

- ***Conscious Luck Morning and Evening Activation Meditation Recordings:*** These three-minute meditations should be listened to daily—once in the morning, and once right before sleep.
- ***Self-Assessment Tool and Focus Guide:*** The Conscious Luck Self-Assessment Tool and Focus Guide allows you to assess where you are on the luck spectrum and exactly how much Conscious Luck you're creating for yourself right now.
- ***Belly-Breath Demonstration Video***: Watch Gay demonstrate belly-breathing in this step-by-step instructional video. This will help you feel more confident using the technique in the many exercises throughout the workbook.
- ***Essence Pace Videos***: The practice of Essence Pace was created by Dr. Kathlyn (Katie) Hendricks. You'll find two instructional videos by Katie that will teach you how to move at your Essence Pace, as well as other links to information and discussion about the practice.
- ***Stationary Essence Pace Instruction Sheet***. This is a downloadable PDF of the instructions you'll need to find your stationary essence pace.
- ***Tracking Forms for both the 21-Day Luck Activation Journal and the 30-Day Lucky Life Tracker***: We've included PDFs of blank tracking forms that you can download and print.
- ***The Eight Secrets Preprinted Poster***. If you would rather not make your own Eight Secrets poster or want to have a preprinted one too, you'll find a link to a PDF of the poster that you can download and color in yourself.
- Additional tools and support materials mentioned throughout the workbook, as well as new ones we develop in the future.

Bonuses for Completing the 30-Day Tracker

Once you have completed 27 - 30 days of Lucky Life tracking, go to www.consciousluck.com/goalachievement to collect your special bonuses and gifts for having taken consistent action.

Advanced Trainings

For information about upcoming advanced trainings, including our e-course on Conscious Luck, visit www.consciousluck.com.

Conscious Luck Videos, Podcasts, and Articles

Recordings of video and audio interviews by Gay and Carol, as well as links to articles in newsletters, magazines, and online publications, are located at https://www.consciousluck.com/media/. You can also read articles written by Gay and Carol at https://www.consciousluck.com/articles/. These resources provide a wonderful opportunity to enhance and expand your understanding of Conscious Luck as Gay and Carol explore and discuss the topic from many different angles.

Recommended Meditation Programs

In Chapter 7, we encouraged you to learn a formal meditation technique and practice it daily to establish a more permanent state of inner calm and stillness. We recommend the following two meditation programs, which Carol and Gay have been practicing for decades—Carol both programs, and Gay the second one. For more information, go to:

1. The Art of Living Foundation's SKY Breath Meditation: https://sky-breath.org/. This is a great technique for people who struggle with meditation or have trouble sitting still.
2. The Transcendental Meditation® Technique: https://www.tm.org/

Join Our Community

Please make sure to join our Global Conscious Luck Community. To do so, please go to https://www.consciousluck.com/facebook and click on the "Join" button at the top of the page. We'd love to see you there; plus you'll receive the most up-to-date information on all things Conscious Luck.

NOTES Section

At the very end of the workbook, we've provided blank pages for you to capture any ideas, drawings, experiences, or insights that you may not have room for in the main part of the workbook. At the top of each page, there's a line for you to write the date. Many people find that it's helpful to include the date of their entries as it allows you to track the different stages of your Conscious Luck growth.

Create an Eight Secrets Poster

We've left the next page blank for you to write out the eight Secrets of Conscious Luck yourself, as recommended at the end of *Conscious Luck*. If you prefer, you can color in the preprinted Eight Secrets poster that's on the page following the blank page. If you want the preprinted poster on a separate piece of paper, you can download it as a PDF through the link on the Conscious Luck workbook website mentioned at the beginning of this section.

Once you complete the Eight Secrets page, we suggest you take a picture of it, print out copies, and tape them to your mirror, refrigerator, or computer screen. Or use the photo of the page as your screensaver or the home-screen image on your tablet or phone. If you'd like, do all of the above—whatever you feel will most effectively keep the Secrets front and center in your life on a daily basis.

THE 8 SECRETS TO INTENTIONALLY
CHANGE YOUR FORTUNE

1. Commit to Be a VLP—Very Lucky Person
2. Release Your Personal Barriers to Good Fortune
3. Transform Shame into a Magnet for Abundance
4. Have Luck-Worthy Goals
5. Take Bold Action Consistently
6. Find Your Lucky Community
7. Learn to Be at the Right Place at the Right Time
8. Practice Radical Gratitude and Appreciation

COMMIT TO BE A VLP
VERY LUCKY PERSON
RELEASE YOUR PERSONAL
BARRIERS TO GOOD FORTUNE
TRANSFORM SHAME
INTO A MAGNET FOR ABUNDANCE
HAVE LUCK-WORTHY GOALS
TAKE BOLD ACTION
CONSISTENTLY
FIND YOUR LUCKY COMMUNITY
LEARN TO BE AT
THE RIGHT PLACE
AT THE RIGHT TIME
PRACTICE RADICAL
GRATITUDE & APPRECIATION

About the Authors

Gay Hendricks

Gay Hendricks, Ph.D., has been a leader in the fields of relationship transformation and body-mind therapies for more than 45 years.

After earning his Ph.D. in counseling psychology from Stanford, Gay served as professor of Counseling Psychology at the University of Colorado for 21 years. He has written more than 40 books, including bestsellers such as *Five Wishes, The Big Leap* and *Conscious Loving* (co-authored with his wife of more than 35 years, Dr. Kathlyn Hendricks). His books have been used as primary texts in universities around the world.

In 2003, Gay co-founded The Spiritual Cinema Circle, which distributes inspirational movies and conscious entertainment to subscribers in 70+ countries.

Gay has offered seminars worldwide and appeared on more than 500 radio and television shows, including OPRAH, CNN, CNBC, and 48 HOURS. In addition to his work with The Hendricks Institute, Gay is currently writing his second mystery series. Learn more about Gay at: https://hendricks.com.

Carol Kline

A #1 *New York Times* bestselling author, Carol has devoted her career to teaching, writing, and speaking about consciousness and personal growth.

Over the last 30 years, Carol has co-authored more than a dozen books with some of the world's top transformational leaders including Jack Canfield and Mark Victor Hansen of *Chicken Soup for the Soul*, Marci Shimoff, Lisa Nichols, and Gay Hendricks. Five of those books have gone on to become *New York Times*, *USA Today*, and *Wall Street Journal* bestsellers.

Her books include *Conscious Luck, Happy for No Reason, Love for No Reason, You've Got to Read this Book, The Ultimate Dog Lover* and *The Ultimate Cat Lover,* as well as five books in the *Chicken Soup for the Soul* series.

Inspired by her experience writing *Chicken Soup for the Pet Lover's Soul* in 1997, she became deeply involved in animal rescue work. This led her to help run and build an animal shelter called Noah's Ark Animal Foundation in Fairfield, Iowa. She was also recently certified as a Climate Reality Leader by Al Gore.

Today, Carol lives in Ojai, California with her husband, Larry, and their dog, Buddy, and is at work on a number of writing, business, and service projects. Learn more about Carol at: https://carolkline.com.

Kamin Samuel

Kamin Samuel is an International Rapid Transformation Business Coach, author, and speaker. A sought-out expert by other coaches and leaders, Kamin specializes in transforming stuck beliefs and behaviors to accelerate growth and high performance. She serves on the faculty of Steve Chandler's Coaching Prosperity School, teaching wealth and success mindset.

She has the distinction of being the U.S. Navy's first African American female helicopter pilot. She has a background in information technology, web development, and online merchandising, and served as the Vice President of Global Website Operations at a billion-dollar company.

Kamin is the award-winning author of *Increase Your Abundance Starting Today!* and the *Wealth Transformation Journal.* Her latest book is the *Success Transformation Journal.*

She is a philanthropist and is especially passionate about assisting educational organizations. She sits on the Board of EduCare Foundation, one of Los Angeles' largest after school program providers, and on the Board of the Internet Marketing Association.

Kamin and her husband, Mark, make their home in Southern California. Learn more about Kamin at: https://kaminsamuel.com.

Date ________________

Date ____________________

Date ________________

Date ____________________

Date ____________________

Date ____________________

Date ____________________

Made in the USA
Las Vegas, NV
31 December 2020

15038241R10144